The Wild Inside

THE WILD INSIDE

Sierra Club's Guide to the Great Indoors

Written and Illustrated by

Linda Allison

Sierra Club Books
San Francisco

Little, Brown and Company
Boston · Toronto · London

The Wild Inside was edited and prepared for publication at The Yolla Bolly Press, Covelo, California.

The Sierra Club, founded in 1892 by John Muir, has devoted itself to the study and protection of the earth's scenic and ecological resources—mountains, wetlands, woodlands, wild shores and rivers, deserts and plains. The publishing program of the Sierra Club offers books to the public as a nonprofit educational service in the hope that they may enlarge the public's understanding of the Club's basic concerns. The Sierra Club has some sixty chapters in the United States and in Canada. For information about how you may participate in its programs to preserve wilderness and the quality of life, please address inquiries to Sierra Club, 730 Polk Street, San Francisco, CA 94109.

Library of Congress Cataloging-in-Publication Data
Allison, Linda.
  The wild inside: Sierra Club's guide to the great indoors / written and illustrated by Linda Allison.
    p.   cm.
  Reprint. Originally published: San Francisco: Sierra Club Books, © 1979.
  Summary: Introduces the basic principles of physics, geology, weather, electricity, and natural history through everyday activities in a house.
  ISBN 0-316-03434-7 (pbk.)
  1. Science—Juvenile literature. [1. Science.] I. Title.
Q163.A44 1988
500—dc19   88-4094
                                                        CIP
                                                         AC
ISBN 0-316-03434-7 (pbk.)
10 9 8 7 6 5 4 3 2
Sierra Club Books/Little, Brown children's books are published by Little, Brown and Company (Inc.) in association with Sierra Club Books.

Many thanks
to Don MacNeil for his help sorting out my indoor insect collection,
to Susan Straight for her kid-tested fireplace recipes,
to Shelly Weinbaum for trying to make snow in the shower,
to Tom MacIntosh for testing his bathtub whirlpool at home in Australia
(even though the results weren't what we expected), and
to David Katz for being the answer man in the science department.

For Mary, who cultivates wildness inside and out
and inspires others to do likewise.

Inside the Wild

Part 3:
Mountains in the House

Part 4:
House Happenings

WARNING: YOU SHOULD ASK FOR ADULT HELP WITH EXPERIMENTS USING FLAMES.

1
Taking Shelter

Part 1
Taking Shelter

Eternal Spring

Where in the world is it? Where do the nights tend toward the cool, but never get cold? Where is the air filled with ever so gentle breezes? Where does the day last as many hours as you like? Where is it never winter and always spring?

A tropical isle? Shangri-la? It is inside your very own house, of course—inside that protected, controlled space we call the indoors. And it's a good thing, because you're a tropical creature.

At Home in the Tropics

Take a good look at yourself. What do you see? No, ignore the baseball hat and the snazzy sneakers with the soles that let you walk up walls and the all-weather vest and the sunglasses. Forget the ear-warmers and the knee protectors that let you fall off your skateboard without getting hurt.

Let's look at you, the basic human creature, without all that protective gear. You are a long, thin, up-right creature that walks with two legs on padded feet. You are hairless except for a patch here and there, most of it quite useless for protection. Very little fur. No feathers. You have the tiniest of scales

covering the tips of your fingers and toes. You have no business living anywhere but in the mildest of climates.

This hairless beast learned long ago that if he was going to get somewhere in this world, he would have to protect himself from the ravages of a hostile en-

13

vironment. He knew that the mission wouldn't be easy and the answers wouldn't come overnight, but eventually he would master the world with a secret weapon called climate control.

Man's first climate control was when he crawled under rocks and ripped the skins off beasts to protect his own. Since then the human mastery of climate control has accomplished the impossible. Fragile human bodies survive daily in such hostile regions as the Arctic snows, the Sahara, and downtown Los Angeles. Climate control has put people on the bottom of the ocean and flying through the upper atmosphere for a routine journey from Pittsburgh to Des Moines, not to mention trips to the moon.

Shelter from What?

Houses have been called machines to live in. Does this seem like an odd thing to say? Well, think about what your house does for you.

First, it acts as your second skin, keeping your outsides at a nice comfortable temperature so that your cells keep chugging along at 98.6 degrees. (Your insides are very particular about the temperature they keep.) Your house also keeps you out of the weather, away from the rain, sleet, wind, and heat.

A house is a safe place to keep your valuables, not just your piggy bank and the TV set, but the really valuable stuff. It keeps the cereal high and dry and the pot roast from being carried away by wild dogs.

A house provides you with protection from predators — mosquitoes and muggers. Think of all the security stuff on the doors.

A house is a private place, the one spot where you can close the door to shut out the noise and the neighbors, a cave to relax in and a snug space in which to sleep.

Shelter Is What and Where You Find It

These places may look wildly different, but they all have one thing in common. They are all shelters that are made to filter the weather outdoors so that the weather inside is tropical, or close to it.

The Dogon people of North Africa live in houses of mud bricks plastered with straw and mud. The roofs are thatched of straw. A family lives in a cluster of buildings. In the hot season everyone sleeps outside.

In parts of China rooms are hollowed out of soil. The soil is loess — rich, deep river silt that is easy to carve. The surface is farmed, and the people live underground.

Hardhat houses called trulli are built in southern Italy. They have plastered walls that are capped with a cone-shaped roof made of flat rocks. The rocks are stacked in place — no cement is used. This way of building has survived since 2000 B.C.

In many places people have found shelter in caves. The cones of Cappadocia in Turkey are man-made caves. Entire villages are carved out of the strange formations of volcanic dust.

Yurts are the felt houses of the wandering Mongolian people of northern Asia. For several thousand years they have lived in these woolen tents stretched over wooden frames.

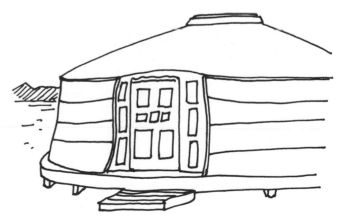

A Masai shepherd's hut is made of brush wood and plastered with cow dung. These nomadic cattle herders of Africa pull apart the hut and take it with them when they move their cattle to a new grazing spot. There is always a good supply of dung where the herds are.

When European settlers came to the Great Plains, they found no trees for building houses. Instead they found endless miles of grasslands. They cut the grass (sod) into hunks and stacked it to make walls. Roofs were added, also of sod.

In the Nebraska sandhill region settlers didn't even find sod. There were only sand dunes with grass. They bailed the grass like hay. The bales, when stacked like bricks, built barns and houses.

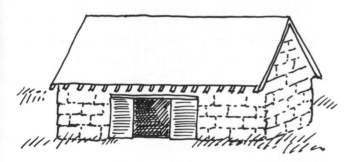

In America it is not uncommon to see trucks that have been converted to shelters. They have light, heat, water, kitchens, sleeping spaces, and even bathrooms sometimes. All the comforts of home. Indeed, for some modern day nomads they are home.

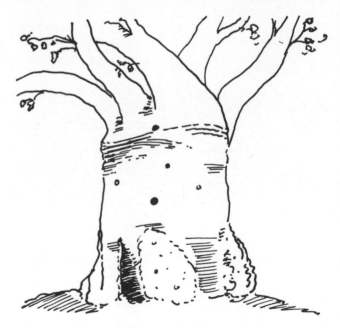

In some parts of Africa the baobab tree trunks grow to be 30 feet across. They are sometimes hollowed out, then people live in the living tree.

Zulu women in Africa build huts by plaiting local grasses. Plaiting, a kind of braiding, is done by hand. These huts last for a long time, and great care is taken to make them beautiful as well as waterproof.

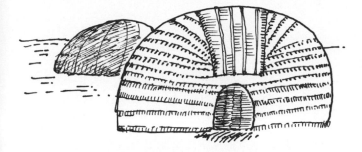

What do you have around your place that you could fashion into a shelter? Nothing? Look around for crates, cardboard, cloth, poles from tree prunings, ropes, string, big leaves, sticks — all of these things are raw materials for shelters.

Under Dog

Under the Australian sun a naked aborigine woman travels and searches for food. With her are her dogs, more than a dozen of them.

When night comes, she lies down to rest. It is cold. Her dogs pile up on her to sleep, their bodies covering hers through the freezing night. In the morning when the sun comes up and her blanket comes to life, she travels to the next water hole with her dog companions.

2
Wild and Not So Wild

Part 2
Wild and Not So Wild

Bats in Your Belfry

Besides all the usual critters that call your house their home, it is not uncommon for a wild creature to take a shine to your shelter—like when swallows nest under your eaves or when you get bats in your belfry or when barn owls move into your garage. There are lots of nooks and crannies around your house that can shelter wild things who come uninvited.

Doves are famous for building makeshift nests in the most unlikely places, like on the front porch or in a hanging flower pot next to the front door.

Squirrels find attics and the under parts of houses nice places to call home. One decided to settle next to the warm water pipes under the deck at my friend Bertha's house. Bertha wasn't sure all that nesting material stuffed next to the pipes was a good idea. It seemed more like a fire waiting to happen. Her solution to this was to discourage the nester with some noise. She turned on a transistor radio full blast to rock 'n' roll music and carefully lowered it down into the squirrel's hideaway. Unfortunately she found that the squirrel liked music. She had to find other means of getting him to leave.

Kamikaze Birds

Thunk. Crash. You go to the window to see who threw the baseball and you notice instead a crumpled pile of feathers under the windowsill. Another bird has bitten the dust. What's the matter with these birds? Why are they trying to kill themselves by flying full force into a window?

21

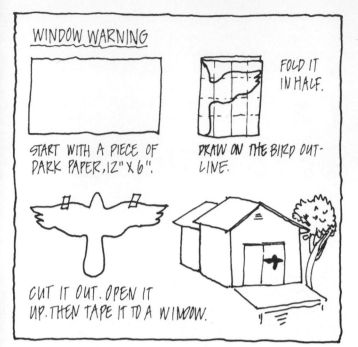

WINDOW WARNING

START WITH A PIECE OF DARK PAPER, 12" X 6".

FOLD IT IN HALF.

DRAW ON THE BIRD OUTLINE.

CUT IT OUT. OPEN IT UP. THEN TAPE IT TO A WINDOW.

lined with cotton or cloth. Let the bird have plenty of support to make it feel secure. Let it rest quietly for half an hour or so. If it is not badly hurt, it will revive in this time. Take care not to make a lot of commotion and scare the bird while it's recovering.

If you have a window that birds crash into, there is a trick you can use to warn them. The silhouette of a predatory bird, such as a hawk, taped to the window should act like a stop sign.

Pets

People have been keeping animals for thousands of years. Probably the first creature kept by humans was the dog. Since then people have tried keeping snakes, hawks, birds that squawk, furry things, animals with scales, monkeys without tails, iguanas, llamas. You name it.

After a lot of trial and error, humans have learned that some animals make much better pets than others. Some creatures have easily adapted to human company. Others, because of their wild natures, remain unwilling captives throughout their entire lives.

What makes the difference? The key is in the mind and behavior patterns of the creature. For instance,

Sometimes the answer is that the bird really mistook the glass for a wide-open space. It just didn't know the window was solid.

What seems to happen more often is that the bird mistakes its own reflection for that of a trespasser in its territory. This often happens during mating season, a time when males are very jealous about their space. The aggressive bird dives into a window, doing its best to chase away a trespasser who turns out to be only a reflection. The result is one stunned bird, or, worse, a bird with a broken neck.

If you come across a bird who has made such a mistake, you might be able to help it. It may have just knocked itself out and will recover in a short while. Meanwhile, it can use some protection from marauding pets. A cat is not inclined to administer first aid in such a situation, but you can.

Gently pick up the bird and move it to a safe, warm place. This might be in the folds of your clothes or wrapped in your hands. You can use a box that is

PLEASE, MOM, CAN I KEEP HIM?

22

bats don't make good pets because their lifestyles don't overlap with human lifestyles. Bats are night creatures. Humans are day creatures, at least most of us are. Unless you are fascinated by sleeping animals that hang around upside down all day, bats are not for you. Besides, it is hard to love a bat.

Rattlesnakes don't make good pets because they are in the habit of injecting poisonous venom into warm mammalian creatures who get close to them. This fact disqualifies rattlesnakes from your list of top ten pets. Besides, it's hard to hug a rattlesnake.

Little green turtles used to be favorite pets. In some states they are now outlawed. That's because they sometimes carry salmonella organisms — bacteria that make humans sick. It's hard to be friendly with an animal that can make you sick.

Lions need big territories and big hunks of meat and, as a result, are expensive to keep. Alligators are damp and not very tidy. The truth is that there are not many animals that adapt well to the indoor life. A good pet is hard to find.

Mighty Mouse

The house mouse is one of the most successful of the indoor wild animals. It is found both in the wild and all over the world as a secret resident of human habitats. House mice are little, weighing not more than an ounce; however, a pair of them can eat up about four pounds of food and deposit 20,000 droppings in a year's time. Under ideal conditions these two mice could produce about 50 young during that year.

Mouse Signs

You may have mice if things mysteriously leap off the shelves at night after the lights are turned off. Mice are most active at dusk and at dawn.

Gnawing, squeaking, scurrying, and rustling are all mouse noises. Gnawing marks and sawdust around the kitchen cabinets and the baseboards are

THE AMAZING HOUSE MOUSE

- IS A GREAT LEAPER AND CAN JUMP 1 FOOT STRAIGHT UP INTO THE AIR.

- CAN JUMP DOWN FROM HIGH PLACES (AS HIGH AS 8 FEET) WITHOUT HURTING ITSELF. AND YOU WONDERED HOW MOUSE TRACKS GOT ON TOP OF THE FRIDGE!

- CAN WALK ALONG A WIRE LIKE A TIGHTROPE WALKER AND CAN RUN UPSIDE DOWN ON MESH.

- CAN SQUEEZE THROUGH OPENINGS BARELY 1/4-INCH WIDE.

- HAS FEET THAT WALK UP WALLS (UNLESS THE WALLS ARE VERY SLICK).

- HAS WHISKERS THAT HELP IT GET AROUND IN THE DARK.

VERY HUNGRY MICE HAVE BEEN KNOWN TO CATCH FLIES FOR FOOD. THEY WILL ALSO MUNCH MOTHS AND BEETLES.

sure signs of mice. A musky odor is produced by mice. Their tracks are footprints and tail marks. Trails in the dust on the floor are mouse signs, so are small, dark droppings.

Mice tend to travel over their territory daily to look for food and to see what is new. Their range is rather small and restricted to a few feet if there is ample food to be found in that area. Mice will eat anything, although their favorites are grains and fatty foods such as cereal and chocolate. The mice in our house collect and store dry cat food and nuts.

Runaway Snake

According to the newspaper article, the lady was putting her breakfast dishes into the dishwasher when she noticed something odd. She closed the door and went on with her chores. Suddenly she realized what she had seen. "My goodness," she yelled, "it's a snake." She mustered her courage, went back to

the dishwasher, and opened the door a crack. Sure enough, there was a snake coiled up in her dishwasher.

It turned out that the apartment had previously been occupied by a belly dancer who used a snake, a python, in her act and that the dancer had lost her snake. One day while she was talking on the phone, the snake had disappeared. She had thought that it had gone down the toilet "as they are always doing." Instead her pet had gone into hibernation under the sink.

What the newspaper article didn't say was that the reunion was happy for the dancer, but the snake was faced with the problem of staying warm in a foreign land. Pythons are tropical animals. They are accustomed to hot, humid places. It was no accident that this creature had curled up in a dishwasher. It was the closest this snake could come to finding a rain forest environment.

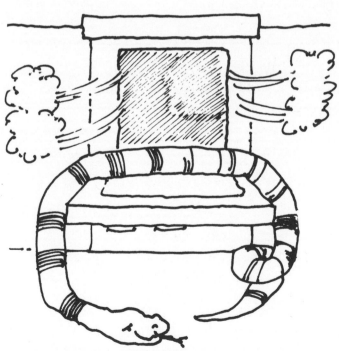

Guide to Once Wild Animals

These animals were not always pets. Once they were wild creatures. They are an international bunch with some interesting histories. Read on to find out some interesting facts about the critters we like to keep.

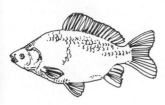

Goldfish. Wild goldfish are not gold. Their real name is carp. The kind we see in pet stores have been bred for their fancy color. Their ancestors came from the streams of China and Japan. Centuries ago the Chinese began to breed them as pets. If returned to the wild, they would revert to plain colors that camouflage them in their natural surroundings. Some goldfish live to be as old as 50 years. In captivity a goldfish will grow to be a few inches in length. Returned to the wild, it may grow to be 12 inches long, adapting its size to the scale of its environment. As many as 20 different varieties of goldfish are commonly sold in pet stores.

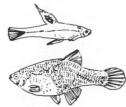

Guppies. Guppies are tropical fish that come from warm South American and West Indian waters. Males are about an inch and a half long, and females are twice that length. Males are rainbow colored and females are silvery. They are useful in some tropical countries because they eat mosquito larvae. A guppy lifetime is three years.

Guinea Pigs. Guinea pig is the name given to a group of furry, South American mammals. Guinea pigs are not pigs,

they are rodents. They were kept as pets by the Incas when the Spanish arrived in the New World in 1500. Dutch traders brought them to Europe. Wild guinea pigs live in burrows in groups of five to ten animals. They are nocturnal vegetarians who whistle when they are scared. They have been hunted for food. Scientists use them for medical research, or as we often say, as guinea pigs.

Gerbils. Another name for the gerbil is kangaroo mouse. This gives you a hint about their talents as leaping creatures. They are relatives of rats. Gerbils are outlaws in California because it is feared that they might escape into crops and wreak havoc. They come from dry, sandy areas of Africa and southwest Asia. Gerbil colonies live underground in tunnels, which they plug during the day to prevent water evaporation. That way they stay cool. Gerbils are fantastic water savers. They get along with the water provided in their diets from seeds and roots. They have water-saving bodies that excrete wastes only in dry form.

Hamsters. Wild hamsters live in deep and elaborate burrows in Europe and western Asia. They are vegetarians. They sleep during the day; at night they gather food, filling their cheeks to carry it back to their tunnels. The first domestic hamster was born at Hebrew University in Israel. A scientist who was studying the sand dunes noticed a family of hamsters burrowing in the soil. He captured some, took them back to his lab, and studied them. Hamsters came to America in 1938.

Dogs. Dogs are the original domestic pet. They have been living with people for about 50,000 years. Their ancestors are either wolves or jackals, or perhaps both of them.

Dogs come in an astounding variety of sizes and shapes. This is the result of human intervention in dog breeding. Every domestic dog has a curly tail, or, at least, one that has a slight curve. Dogs are very social animals who like to live in groups. This makes them good company for humans. Modern dogs suffer from loneliness and depression when left alone.

Cats. The origins of the cat are not known. Egyptians have been keeping them since 3000 B.C. They were protected and worshipped and were valuable creatures in a land where the food supply of grain was in constant danger because of mice. The wild relative of our domestic cat is thought to be the African wildcat, an animal slightly larger than a house cat that still exists in Africa. Cats are nocturnal hunting creatures and not very social. Even though they have been living with people for thousands of years, they still behave like small wild tigers.

Parakeets. These birds are also known as budgerigars, or budgies for short. They are members of the parrot family. Males have blue nostrils. They can learn words, become quite tame, and are natural acrobats.

The wild, Australian kind is green. The birds are also found wild in Africa, India, and Asia. A wild bird known as the Carolina parakeet also lived in America, as far north as New York. The last one seen was in the Florida Everglades in 1904. For a time, hat makers stuffed them and put them on hats. They are now extinct.

Canaries. These birds are really wild finches from the Canary Islands near Spain. They are now alive and singing their hearts out in all parts of the world. Canaries are bred for their song. Domestic birds have prettier songs than their wild cousins, at least to human ears. Canaries have been kept in cages in Europe since Renaissance times.

Send Away: Pet Poster

How about a big colorful poster that tells all about how to care for your pet? It has facts about feeding and housing and tips on how to keep a cat, dog, guinea pig, rabbit, horse, tropical fish, caged bird, hamster, mouse, and rat. Send two dollars to:

The Animal Protection Institute of America
P.O. Box 22505
Sacramento, California 95822

Cat Walk

Have you ever been out for a walk with your cat? Unlike a dog, a cat doesn't generally go for walks with people. Sometime you might go out for a walk with your cat. Don't expect him to stick close to your heels. A cat doesn't like traveling with another creature as the leader. Rather, you will have to let your cat take the lead. Get ready to go slowly. Notice how a cat takes care crossing open spaces. Follow your cat quietly, letting him choose the direction. Get ready to climb fences and crawl through hedges. Notice what he sees, how he pauses and sniffs the breeze. You may start out following a pussy cat, but after a while you may decide you are tailing a domestic tiger.

Dog, the Domestic Success

Why does your dog sit at your feet and look lovingly at you? How come your dog gets wildly excited when you get home from school? It is because the dog is a domestic animal *par excellence*. Dogs love to be loved by people. Dogs are very social creatures and after thousands of years of selective breeding by people, dogs have become convinced they are man's best friend.

Dogs have personalities that are easily adapted to life with man. They are pack animals. That means they generally follow a leader animal. It is a short step for a canine to adopt a human for his pack leader. It is easy for them to remain dependent for life on their human masters.

Why doesn't your kitty jump up and lick your face when you get home from school? Cats are domestic pets too. Even though a cat lives happily in human company, it remains a solitary hunting creature. Cats are stealthy and quick. They are deadly hunters who enjoy the night. Cat nature is quite different from dog nature. No amount of domestic life can change that.

How Come Bulldogs Wheeze?

If you have ever stood next to a bulldog, you know that they wheeze when they breathe. That's because their faces are flat, and there isn't quite enough room in their breathing apparatus for air to circulate easily. Some bulldogs have choked to death on their own soft palates. This problem is shared by Pekingese, pugs, and other dogs with flattened faces.

Why do bulldogs have flat faces? This sad state of affairs started around 1850 with the invention of the dog show. Before this time dogs were bred for skills like herding or hunting.

A dog show is a beauty contest. Like any other beauty contest it's all looks, brains don't count. If a breed of bulldog is supposed to have a flat face, breeders will compete with each other to produce the animal with the flattest one.

Beauty has always been hard to explain. Be thankful that the people who are in charge of beauty aren't in charge of evolution.

Bulldogs

Bull baiting was a sport that pitted dog against bull. Dogs were trained to go for the bull's throat and to hang on until the bull came to its knees. Gentlemen sat on the sidelines, betting on the outcome. It is probably because of this sport that bulldogs were first bred to have flat faces. Some dog breeder must have reasoned that a dog with a short snout could get a better grip on a bull's throat. That is a strange reason to breed a dog with a flat nose, but it is probably no stranger than some of the other reasons for which dogs have been bred.

Send Away: Pet First Aid

Do you know how to give your dog medicine? Or how to carry an injured animal? Or where to find a cat's pulse? Or what to do when your dog swallows a pin cushion? There is a very handy booklet that tells you the answers to these questions, plus what to do for poisonings, shock, and broken bones. It is full of good pictures to help you with animal emergencies. If you are a pet owner, you should know some animal first aid. Send for "The Angell Memorial Guide to Animal First Aid." Send $1.25 to:

Massachusetts Society for the
   Prevention of Cruelty to Animals
350 South Huntington Avenue
Boston, Massachusetts 02130

THE LOGIC OF DOGS' BODIES

DACHSHUNDS' LOW-SLUNG, LOOSE-SKINNED BODIES ARE PERFECT FOR CRAWLING INTO BADGER BURROWS.

TERRIERS WERE BRED TO BE RAT CATCHERS.

POINTERS ARE BRED WITH THE TALENT OF FREEZING IN POSITION WHEN THEY SENSE GAME.

GREYHOUNDS ARE BUILT FOR SPEED.

TOY BREEDS ARE BRED FOR HOUSE PETS. THE GREEKS RAISED LAP DOGS, WHICH WERE MEANT TO KEEP LADIES' STOMACHS WARM.

BASSETS ARE BIG-NOSED TRACKERS. THEIR SHORT LEGS ARE SO PEOPLE ON FOOT CAN KEEP UP WITH THEM.

Send Away:
Pause for Paws

A lot of kids like having animals around the house. You can put more animals in your life with some animal posters for your walls. "Be Kind to One and All" is a color-it-yourself poster with a variety of whimsical animals. It costs 25 cents. "Living with Animals" shows people and animals living together in homes, apartments, a zoo farm, and forest. It costs 50 cents and is also a poster for you to color yourself.

Crossing streets can be dangerous for kids and for small animals. You can help remind drivers to watch out for dogs, cats, and other small creatures with a bumper sticker that says, "Pause for Paws." It is available in either blue or orange and costs 75 cents.

Add 25 cents with each order for postage. Write to:

Publications Department
Massachusetts Society for the Prevention of
    Cruelty to Animals
350 South Huntington Avenue
Boston, Massachusetts 02130

Creatures Who Live
on Creatures

There are all sorts of small creatures who live on bigger ones. There is a special name for those who make a living taking bites out of their hosts. The word is *parasite*. Most plants and animals have parasites of some kind. Even some parasites have parasites.

Usually a parasite is a lot smaller than its host. At some stage in a parasite's life it feeds on its host, but generally it doesn't take big bites. It is not in a parasite's best interest to be too greedy. They are small, so it's unlikely that a few parasites will do much harm. Problems arise when the size of the parasite population increases. A thoroughly colonized host can get sick and die.

Life on Dog

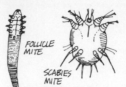

Mites. Tiny microscopic mites can colonize a dog and cause itching skin called mange. There are several kinds. One is a cigar-shaped beast that burrows in hair follicles (the area where the hair grows out of the skin). Another type is a spider-shaped mite that lives on skin — of dogs and people.

Ticks. These bloodsuckers work their way into a dog's skin, especially around the neck and ears. They are picked up in woods and fields. Male ticks look like small, dark seeds. Females get to be swollen and blue gray in color after a meal. They drop off to lay their eggs in protected cracks and corners.

You have probably never thought of your dog as a nice warm place to live. There are many creatures who do. In fact, your dog might be playing host to a whole population of small creatures. Where? Both on his inside and outside. Here is a guide to what might hide on or in your dog's hide.

Worms. There are hookworms, whipworms, roundworms, and tapeworms. These worms do not live on the dog, but reside inside the dog's intestines. They make a living by robbing the dog of food it has eaten. Some of these worms also eat blood. They appear in dog droppings and can be seen with the aid of a microscope.

Fleas. These are small, brownish insects with hind legs well developed for leaping. These insects move around on the dog's surface. Fleas hop off to lay their eggs in bedding, cracks, carpets, and other warm, damp spots.

Ringworm. These are not worms. They are fungi that can colonize skin (human skin too). They are tiny, and colonies of them show up as red rings that itch.

Lice. They can live their whole lives attached to the surface of a dog. First, they are eggs that are stuck onto the dog's hair. Then they hatch and attach themselves to the dog's skin, feeding on its blood.

Parasite Rhyme

So, Nat'ralists observe, a Flea
Hath smaller Fleas that on him prey.
And those have smaller Fleas to bite 'em
And so proceed ad infinitum.

A man clearly interested in little beings and worlds within worlds wrote this poem that is a favorite of ecologists. His name was Jonathan Swift. He is the author of *Gulliver's Travels*.

Parasites are such a common occurrence in the animal world that the only creatures sure to be free of them are the tiniest parasites—maybe those that live on the fleas themselves.

Who Is Pestering Whom?

Termites have a bad reputation. They are considered evil creatures bent on the destruction of innocent people's houses. People have spent a lot of money figuring out ways to get rid of termites. Nobody likes a termite.

Think for a minute of the termite in a different light. Who is this evil creature? Termites have been around for millions of years. During this time they have learned how to make a living eating wood. That is a good trick since cellulose is an undigestible, inedible food to most creatures. Termites have lived successful lives in most warm parts of the world, wherever wood has been in supply. Termites, along with various fungi and molds, make sure the forest floors of the world don't get cluttered with stacks of dead trees and limbs. After all, if the old trees didn't break down, there would be no room for new ones.

Termites do what they always have done, get along eating wood. This was a perfectly happy state of natural affairs until people decided tree bodies are the perfect material for building houses. Look at it from a termite's point of view. We live in houses built out of termite lunches. Now who is the pest? It's really a matter of your point of view.

Instant Insect Collection

Right now in your house there is a good chance that you have a rather splendid insect collection.

No? Think again. Have you overlooked the light fixtures? If they haven't been cleaned in a while, there are, no doubt, some insects lying there waiting to be inspected. Since they are already dead, you won't have to kill them to keep them still while you look at them.

MOST OF THE INSECTS YOU FIND WILL BE ONES THAT ARE ATTRACTED TO LIGHT. THE CLIMATE, SEASON, AND YOUR LOCAL ENVIRONMENT WILL AFFECT YOUR CATCH.

Look around your house for lamps that have open sides where a bug could fly into the light bulb. The lights that hang from the center of the room are good places to look. So are the ones that screw into the ceiling or over the medicine cabinet. Get permission and some help if these are in hard-to-reach places. Shake out your finds onto a sheet of paper. You can get a box if you want to keep them for identification.

Positive Identification

If you want to get to know your bugs by their first names, you will need to get an insect guide. There are about a zillion kinds of insects, and even the experts have a difficult time telling precisely what bug they are looking at.

Don't be discouraged. You will be able to tell the wasps from the weevils, and you will discover a lot of fascinating information along the way. Field guides to insects are reference books that your library probably has. A good insect guide has pictures that will help you pick out the family your creatures belong to.

General Guide to Inside Insects

Silverfish. These silver-colored insects are about one-half inch long. They are carrot-shaped, quite primitive, and have no wings. Their bodies are covered with tiny scales, which give them a flashy appearance. They are sometimes called bristletails because of their long, hairlike tails.

Look for them at night. During the day they hide in cracks and crevices and in the corners of drawers. You might spot them outdoors in warm weather. Silverfish don't do a lot of damage, although they horrify most housekeepers. They like to chew anything with starch in it, like glue or flour. They have been seen nibbling wallpaper, bookbindings, clothes, and cereals.

Clothes Moths. There are two kinds of moths that commonly chew holes in your sweaters. The webbing clothes moth is a golden buff creature about one-quarter inch long. The casemaking clothes moth is drab with dark spots. The larvae are the hungry creatures that do the damage to your woollies. These are pearly white, wormlike creatures with naked bodies and dark heads.

The casemaking clothes moth likes to conceal itself in the folds of clothes. It builds a silken burrow where it hides when it is disturbed. It likes dark closets and doesn't like being disturbed. Besides wool it eats pollen, fur, feathers, and insect remains.

An entire generation of moths can mature in a month in a dark, quiet closet with a good food supply. The eggs will hibernate at temperatures below 40 degrees. The moral is to keep your winter clothes in the refrigerator.

Carpet Beetles. These are small, handsome beetles that look somewhat like a dark brown version of a ladybug. You will see them mostly in the spring when they migrate outside to eat pollen.

It is the larvae that eat carpets, not to mention hooves, horns, hair, and feathers. When their favorite diet of dead animal covers is not available, they will resort to cereals. Then you might see these mottled black-and-brown larvae in the kitchen. The eggs are sometimes found in furniture, especially where lint collects. Bird nests and animal beds are also favorite spots.

Roaches. There are four kinds of roaches commonly found in North American houses. Each has habits and descriptions that are different.

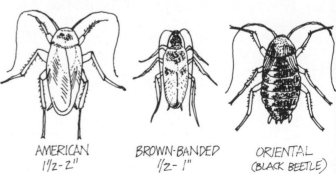

AMERICAN
1½-2"

BROWN-BANDED
½-1"

ORIENTAL
(BLACK BEETLE)

The American roach is light brown in color and has reddish wings. It may be found almost anywhere in the house.

The Oriental roach is sometimes called the black beetle. It has a very dark shiny body. It loves dark, damp spaces. You will run into it under houses, in sod, and in leaves and vegetation.

The brown-banded roach is the high and dry member of the everyday-around-the-house roaches. You will recognize it by the light and dark bands on its body. It hangs out in cupboards, shelves, inside motors, and behind pictures. It has even been found living inside radios.

The German roach is also known as the Croton Bug. It was first discovered in the Croton Aqueduct in New York City. This roach was imported from Europe. It likes damp places such as gutters and bathrooms.

The German roach is probably the most common type of roach in America. The Germans, however, call it the French roach. Originally it apparently migrated to Europe by way of Asia, stowed away in a folded tent or saddlebag.

All roaches might have originally come from Africa. The semitropical inside of the human house makes a good substitute for the African climate. Roaches have been living with humans for as long as anyone can remember. There are 3,500 kinds, most of which live in tropical climates.

Roaches give off a musky smell that bothers tidy housekeepers. They are omnivorous and have a taste for things such as fabrics, books, wallpaper, and human foods. Their legs are built for running fast, and they are expert at hiding in tiny cracks.

Fleas. Fleas are small but mean. They are hard-bodied creatures with big legs and a tiny head. They have a flattened body that is brown or blackish with no wings. Fleas don't need wings because their remarkable jumping ability gets them where they want to go, which is usually on a warm-blooded mammal. If you could jump like a flea, you could leap about 500 feet straight up — like jumping up to the fortieth floor of a skyscraper.

The mouthparts of fleas are made for sucking blood. Unfortunately fleas carry germs and bacteria, and they can transmit these unwelcome travelers to the creatures they bite. Fleas have been responsible for some of the world's worst plagues and epidemics. Historians have said that Napoleon's army wasn't stopped by the British but by the armies of fleas that infested his troops. Fleas live on furniture, clothing, and the family dog and cat.

Flies. The most common type of fly in your house is probably the *Musca domestica* — the grayish black fly that is about one-quarter inch long. This creature breeds in kitchen garbage, lawn clippings, and other decomposing rubbish. Its favorite breeding place is in horse manure, and in the days of stables and horse transportation, flies were much more common.

Flies have their tasters on their feet, and they are fond of human food as well as the rotting bits that we throw away. A housefly is a living zoo and can carry as many as 33 million microorganisms in its gut—one-half million more might live on its hairy surface. When it walks over your picnic food, it doesn't walk alone. That fact and its habit of hanging out in dung heaps make it an undesirable guest to be tracking anything you plan to eat.

In two weeks a fly may lay 1000 eggs that can mature to maggots, then pupae, then adult flies in warm weather. This accounts for the population explosion among flies in the summer. In a warm environment flies can breed all year long. If you live in a city, the fly on your window probably was born on your block, although flies can travel a couple of miles. They cruise at about five miles per hour.

Blowflies. These flies are sometimes known as bottle flies. They are the heavy-duty ones with the shiny metallic bodies in green and blue. These flies lay their eggs in decaying meat or in the sores of animals.

 *Fruit Flies.* Scientists call this fly *Drosophila.* It is a small, light brown or yellowish fly that is about one-eighth inch long or less. It has bright red eyes and mouthparts designed for lapping up the juices of fermenting fruits. You might see some hanging around the bruised bananas or overripe oranges in the fruit bowl. Scientists are fascinated with this fly because of its ability to produce a new generation in only eight to twelve days. Because it has giant chromosomes (carriers of genetic information), the fruit fly has taught us a lot about genetics.

INSECTS IN THE HOUSE ARE NOT ALWAYS CONSIDERED A PROBLEM. IN MEXICO HONEY ANTS ARE A SWEET TREAT SERVED ON SPECIAL OCCASIONS.

Little House Flies. These are the flies that seem to spend all their time in the air. They hang out in the middle of the room and seldom land.

House Crickets. The house cricket is a tan insect with dark bands about three-quarters inch long. They are also called cave or camel crickets. They stand on long legs and sport long antennae that sweep back the entire length of their bodies.

This kind of cricket likes warm, dark places such as basements and crawl spaces under the house. Sometimes they live just outside and dine on whatever they find attractive. Indoors crickets are omnivorous and will eat things such as wool rugs, wallpaper paste, the glue in bookbindings, drapes, and leftovers from the garbage can. If you are hoping for cricket music from this fellow, you will be disappointed. House crickets don't sing.

Face-to-Face with a Fly

After learning about all the things that cling to the bodies of flies, you most probably won't want to get close to one. If you can conquer your fear and wash your hands afterwards, you can find out some interesting things by having a face-to-face encounter with the dead fly you find on the windowsill.

There is a simple way of making a stand that will let you handle the fly without having to touch its body. It is a good trick to know if you are planning to look at insects since they are fragile and break easily. To make the stand you will need:

    some Plasticine clay
    some little pieces of cardboard
    some straight pins

SPEAR THE INSECT FROM UNDERNEATH.

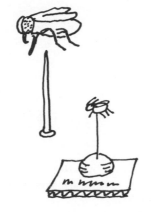

ROLL A SMALL BALL OF CLAY. STICK THE HEAD OF THE PIN INTO THE CLAY.

PRESS THE CLAY ONTO THE CARDBOARD.

WRITE IDENTIFICATION NOTES ON THE CARDBOARD STAND OR CUT A PAPER STRIP LABEL.

START A COLLECTION.

Fly Bodies

Buzzzzzzzz Sfft thunk zzzzzzzz

How is it that a fly can zoom across a room at top speed, crash into a window, then get up a second later to do the same thing all over again? Why is it that flies don't seem to feel a thing?

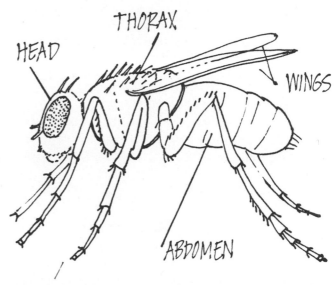

REMEMBER, INSECTS ALWAYS HAVE SIX LEGS.

The secret is in their suit.

A fly, like all insects, wears its bones on the outside, which makes it immune to head-on crashes into glass windows. How does an insect make sense of the world if it lives inside an armored plate? Insects are covered with sensory hairs. These hairs act like fingers and are sensitive to motion and wind. An insect feels the world through the hairs on its surface.

The fly's body comes in three parts—standard equipment for the entire insect world. First, there is a head on the forward end. Next, comes the chest part or *thorax*. Bringing up the rear is the section called the abdomen. Attached to the basic insect body is a set of legs. Insect legs always come in sets of six. If you are not sure what you have is an insect, you can take a leg count. The fly has a nice set of transparent wings attached to its thorax. Insect wings come in all sizes and shapes. Some flies have two pairs, and some insects such as fleas don't need any wings at all.

Looking at your fly through a magnifying glass, you might be shocked to discover that he is quite a hairy beast. He sports not just a lot of little hairs, but long stiff hairs all over his body. This is one reason the fly is so wise to the approach of a swatter. The hairs on his body tip him off by sensing the blast of air. These hairs also help him to fly in a straight line.

Look again and you will see that his eyes take up most of his tiny head. They are actually clusters of eyes. Flies have the ability to see what is in front of them and behind them as well. If you had eyes like the fly, you would be a rather strange-looking person.

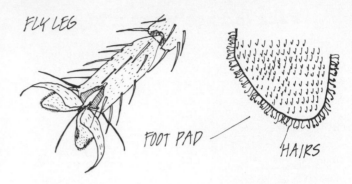

FLY LEG

FOOT PAD

HAIRS

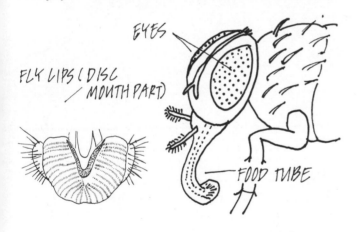

EYES

FLY LIPS (DISC MOUTH PART)

FOOD TUBE

There are two basic insect diets. One is solid and the other is liquid food. The result is that in the insect world there are two basic types of lips: hard, horny mouthparts that are made for chewing and mouthparts that are made for sucking. Flies suck and have the mouthparts of a sucker. However, the end of their food tube is a disc that is rough, like a file. With this the fly is able to scrape up small crumbs, which are then sucked into his food tube.

Fly feet are outstanding inventions. Not only can a fly walk up walls, he can taste the wallpaper along the way. That's right, a fly's tasters are on his tootsies. A fly's foot consists of two claws. Between them is a little pad that is covered with sticky hairs. These hairs are the reason that a fly can walk up windows and across ceilings. These feet are also wonderful catchers for all sorts of microlife that they run across. And, as you know, flies are constantly sticking their feet in unhealthy places. That is why you now need to wash your hands if you have been handling one.

Fly Notes

Flies make a tremendous amount of noise for their size. Imagine what sort of sound a dog-size fly would make. It is too horrible to contemplate. How do they do it?

The common housefly hums around the room at F note. Its wings set up a vibration of 345 cycles per second, which is just about middle F on the piano. A fly beats its wings at 20,700 times per minute. Knowing that a higher note means more vibrations per second, do a mosquito's wings beat faster or slower than those of a fly?

Active bees produce a note of A (435 cycles per second), while a tired bee hums along at E (326 cycles per second). Mad or belligerent bees move up the scale.

Insect Amplifier

With some very simple stuff you can make a little chamber that will magnify insect sounds. Try it with a couple of different insects and hum along. This amplifier will also let you clearly hear bug footsteps.

1. Find a paper cup, a sheet of thin paper, and a rubber band.

2. Capture the insect you want to listen to in the cup.

3. Place the paper over the top of the cup and fold over the edge. Hold it in place with a rubber band.

4. Hold the amplifier to your ear and listen in. This may be the first time you have ever bugged an insect.

YOU WILL NEED

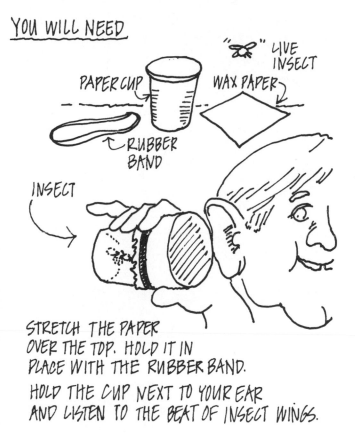

STRETCH THE PAPER OVER THE TOP. HOLD IT IN PLACE WITH THE RUBBER BAND.

HOLD THE CUP NEXT TO YOUR EAR AND LISTEN TO THE BEAT OF INSECT WINGS.

Itsy-Bitsy Spider

Spiders appear in the most unlikely spots. Right now one is hanging from the lamp suspended over my desk. It is about the size of a semicolon and appears to be building a web, leaping off the edge of the lamp, then knitting its way back up, twirling around in a death-defying fashion.

Small as it is, it has all the regular spider body parts. All spiders have eight legs. (Insects have six.) They also have a two-part body. The front part is called the cephalothorax (your friends should be impressed with that word), which is followed by an abdomen. The two sections are joined by a thin stalk, which contains some important spider mechanisms such as the aorta, the intestines, the main nerve

WOULD YOU BELIEVE THAT SPIDERS HAVE BEEN SOLD IN FRANCE FOR USE IN WINE CELLARS AS A SUBSTITUTE FOR FLY PAPER!

But Everybody Calls Me Harry

HI, MY NAME IS HAROLD PEACHTREE, BUT MY FRIENDS CALL ME HARRY.

I'M DAN DOVER, BUT SCIENTISTS CALL ME HOMO SAPIENS.

cord, and some muscles. At the rear of the abdomen on the underside are some faucetlike organs called spinnerets, which produce silk for spider webs. The opposite end of the spider is equipped with jaws that sport a pair of fangs. These fangs contain poison glands. (Only a few spiders have poison fangs that can hurt humans.) Spiders, like insects, wear their bones on the outside. They have hard shells on their bodies and soft insides. A lot of spiders are covered with sensory hairs.

Naturalists are forever speaking about tiny creatures with names a mile long in a foreign language. Why bother with all that Latin stuff?

The problem with the common everyday names is that they don't mean the same thing to everybody. Consider, for example, the critter that is commonly called daddy longlegs. Some people call the harvestman a daddy longlegs; others call the long-legged spider daddy longlegs; there are still others who call all spiders with long legs daddy longlegs.

This sort of thing can get really confusing. That's when the Latin name comes in handy. Biologists give each creature on earth a first and last name in Latin so we can tell precisely which creature we are talking about. The following spider guide includes Latin names so that you can look up these creatures in other books if you want to learn more about them. That way you're sure who's who.

Remember, you don't have to be Latin to use Latin names.

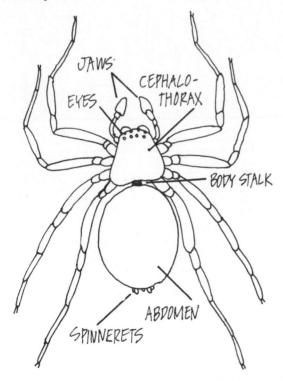

JAWS

EYES

CEPHALO-THORAX

BODY STALK

ABDOMEN

SPINNERETS

Spider Guide

Brown Spiders (*Loxosceles reclusa*). These spiders are also called the brown recluse and they live in sheltered places such as inside houses. Their favorite spots are on floors and behind furniture. Their webs are sheets of sticky silk. These cobweb weavers suck their prey dry after first binding them in silk. The male spider courts the female by visiting her web and plucking its threads.

Daddy Longlegs (*Pholcus phalangioides*). These are the spiders that look like they are on stilts. They are common indoors. You will see them hanging around upside down

in quiet corners of houses and basements. They travel rapidly with a long, awkward gait. Males and females are often found together. The female carries egg sacs in her mouth.

Harvestmen (*Phalangium opilio*). These are sometimes confused with daddy longleg spiders. Harvestmen are not true spiders, although they are very close relatives. You can tell they are not spiders by their segmented abdomen, their lack of a waist, and their very long legs. If your legs were as long in relation to your body length as the harvestman's legs are to its body, you would be about 40 feet tall. If you have ever tried to capture one, you know that the harvestman's legs have a tendency to break off easily. You may have noticed one with a short leg—it is growing a replacement for a leg lost along the way.

Generally you won't see harvestmen indoors unless one wanders in by accident. They are at home in the fields where they feed on insects and plant juices. They got their name from the fact that so many are seen during harvest when they run for their lives over leaves and grass to avoid the harvest machinery.

Widows (*Lactrodectus*). These are the biggest and best known of the cobweb weavers. They are famous (maybe *infamous* is a better word here!) for their bite and for the female's habit of eating her mate.

The black widow (*Lactrodectus mactans*) is found in most parts of the United States. It lives in out-of-the-way spots like piles of wood, outhouses, basements, and garages. The female black widow has a red hourglass shape on her belly.

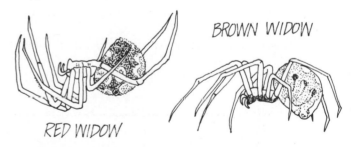

RED WIDOW

BROWN WIDOW

Cousins of the black widow who live in North America include brown widow (*Lactrodectus geometricus*), red widow (*Lactrodectus bishopi*), and northern widow (*Lactrodectus variolus*). All have poisonous bites. You aren't likely to see these others indoors. The first two live in hot spots such as Florida. The northern widow is found mostly in the woods.

THE HARVESTMAN IS ALSO KNOWN AS THE QUIVER OR SHIMMY SPIDER BECAUSE IT "HIDES" BY SHAKING ITSELF UP AND DOWN IN ITS WEB.

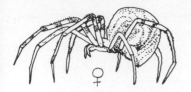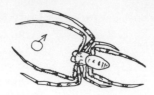

American House Spiders (*Achaearanea tepedariorum*). These common spiders are cobweb weavers. You might find them around your house hanging upside down in irregular webs or hiding in a crevice.

Spider Bites

In North America there are just two kinds of spiders that have a dangerous bite. Spiders are not dangerous beasts. They bite only as a last resort. Even then they have to work hard to puncture your tough hide with their fangs. Mostly bites happen when you get too close to a spider for comfort.

One of the spiders with a nasty bite is the brown recluse. This is the one that usually lives underfoot on the floor or behind furniture. If one bites you, you might get some red swelling around the bite area. If you have a severe reaction, you get a scab that takes a couple of months to heal. Or nothing at all may happen.

Black widows and their kin are the other spiders you don't want to squeeze. Nothing happens around the bite area; in fact, you might not notice anything

at all. Later you might feel as if you have appendicitis, sore soles of the feet, and swollen, aching muscles. A person usually recovers in a few days.

There is no first aid for a spider bite, but if you feel you might have fallen victim to one of these fanged creatures, see your doctor.

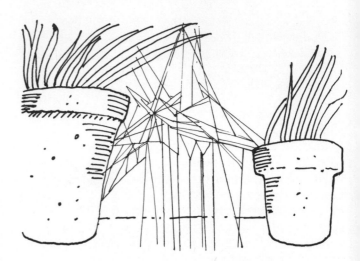

Looking at Webs

Have you ever wondered what a spider eats for lunch? One way to find out is to look for yourself. A spider web sometimes resembles a meat locker. These silken snares occasionally hold wall-to-wall bound and hung insect bodies of all shapes and sizes.

Look for webs in the quiet, undisturbed places in your house—under the bathroom sink, by the hot water heater, in the garage. You know where to look for spiders.

When you find a web, gently nudge the spider out of the way so you can look at the web. You might want to take it down and press it against a sheet of paper. It will stick easily. See how many insect bodies there are and how many different kinds. Check back later to see how long it takes your spider to build a new web.

IN PARIS AT THE WORLD'S FAIR OF 1900, CURTAINS MADE OF SPIDER SILK WERE DISPLAYED. 25,000 SPIDERS CONTRIBUTED TO THE 18-YARD LENGTH.

SPIDER CAGE

THESE ARE GOOD FOR GETTING A CLOSE LOOK. USE A JAR. PUNCH HOLES IN THE LID. GROUND SPIDERS WILL NEED SOME GROUND. AERIAL SPIDERS NEED A TWIG FOR THEIR WEBS. SPIDERS WILL NEED A BIT OF DAMPNESS IN THEIR CAGE, BUT DON'T LET IT GET MOLDY. TRY FEEDING THEM MEALYBUGS. SPIDERS ARE CANNIBALS, SO YOU WILL WANT TO KEEP YOUR EIGHT-LEGGED FRIENDS SEPARATE.

SPIDER WATCH

KEEP WATCH ON A SINGLE SPIDER IN YOUR HOUSE. HOUSE SPIDERS HAVE SMALL TERRITORIES, SO YOU CAN VISIT THE SAME SPOT AND EXPECT TO FIND IT HOME. NOTICE WHAT IT EATS. WATCH FOR MOLTING. SEE IF YOU CAN TELL IF IT'S A MALE OR A FEMALE. IF YOUR HOUSE HAS MORE THAN AN OCCASIONAL SPIDER, WATCH FOR MATING. YOU MIGHT NOTICE A FEMALE CARRYING AN EGG. WATCH FOR SPIDER BABIES.

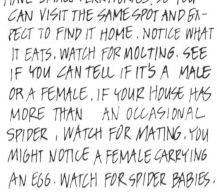

CATCH A SPIDER

FIND THE SPIDER YOU WANT TO STUDY. LOOK FOR THEM IN CORNERS.

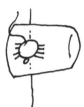

COVER THE SPIDER WITH A GLASS. BE CAREFUL NOT TO HARM IT.

SLIDE A SHEET OF PAPER UNDER THE GLASS.

MOVE THE CRITTER TO A SPIDER CAGE.

SPIDER SIGNS

SPIDER SKINS LOOK LIKE DEAD SPIDERS, BUT LOOK CLOSELY AND YOU WILL SEE THEY ARE EMPTY. LIKE SNAKES, SPIDERS MOLT. THEY BREAK OUT OF THEIR SKIN WHEN IT GETS TOO TIGHT. THEY WILL MOLT 4-12 TIMES BEFORE THEY'RE FULL GROWN.

<u>INSECT MUMMIES</u> - THESE ARE SILK-WRAPPED HUSKS OF INSECTS (OR LITTER LEFT OVER FROM A SPIDER LUNCH).

WEBS

ARE SPUN OF SPIDER SILK, THE STRONGEST FIBER FOUND IN NATURE. EACH TYPE OF SPIDER SPINS ITS OWN SPECIAL KIND OF WEB FROM SILK GLANDS (SPINNERETS) AT THE REAR OF ITS BODY. SPIDERS USE SILK TO BUILD TRAPS, HOMES, PARACHUTES, AND SLINGS FOR THEIR EGGS. MOST INDOOR SPIDERS BUILD IRREGULAR WEBS CALLED COBWEBS.

In addition to insects in the web, you might find some whitish spider bodies. These are the spider's old bones. When a spider grows bigger, its hard outer skeleton becomes too tight, so the spider sheds its suit of armor. Before this happens the inside layers of the skeleton are digested, then the outer skin splits and the spider steps out of it with motions that are something like a person wriggling out of a pair of tight jeans. A spider sheds its skin four to twelve times before it reaches adult size.

Adopt a Spider

Spiders are interesting critters. They don't bark, shed, or infect the living room rug with fleas. Besides that they are interesting critters that can easily be at home in an empty jar. If keeping a wild animal in captivity is against your principles, you can adopt an indoor spider to keep tabs on.

Spiders eat insects. They do this the way you might drink a milkshake with the lid on. Pretend that the two straws are fangs the spider sticks through the skin of the insect to suck out the juice — the same way you sip a milkshake without taking off the lid. The difference is that you don't inject your milkshake with a dose of poison to paralyze it so it won't put up a fight or walk away.

What a Mold Is

Hunger strikes. You go to the refrigerator and pull out a carton of cottage cheese. You rip off the lid. You dig in. The spoon comes up, your mouth opens, the sour smell hits your nose. You look to see what's wrong. There are spots all over the stuff. You put the lid on quickly and dump the whole thing in the garbage, probably before you noticed much about the creatures who beat you to the cottage cheese.

It's the normal reaction. People are either disgusted or furious that a mold should have the gall to show up in their cottage cheese. They forget to be fascinated by these creatures that can live in a refrigerator. People forget to wonder how mold can colonize a cheese that is kept under cover or to think about how long it has been there or how it knew where to go to find cottage cheese to eat in the first place.

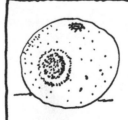

DID YOU KNOW THE GREEN SPOTS ON ROTTEN ORANGES ARE PENICILLIN MOLD, THE SAME STUFF FROM WHICH THE WONDER DRUG IS MADE?

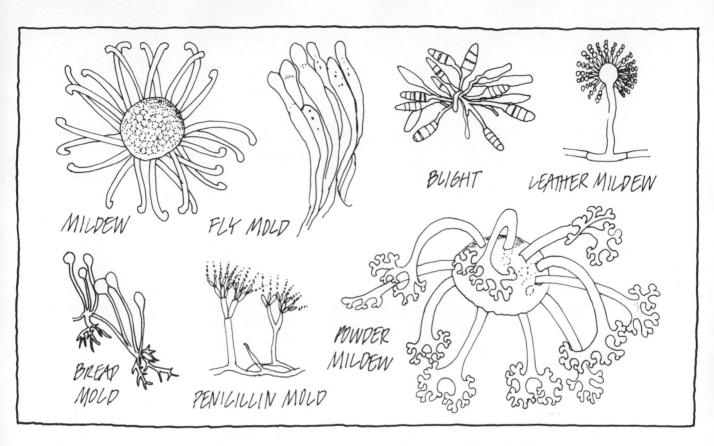

MILDEW   FLY MOLD   BLIGHT   LEATHER MILDEW

BREAD MOLD   PENICILLIN MOLD   POWDER MILDEW

We think of molds as malicious beasts bent on destroying food in our refrigerators. Not so. Molds are microscopic plants doing their best to get along just like the rest of us. Think of them as uninvited house plants or indoor weeds on a microscopic scale.

A mold is a tiny plant, a special kind of plant that lives directly on its dinner. Unlike green plants, molds do not make their own food from sunlight, so they must find food and set up shop right on its surface. Whole forests of these microplants grow on food wherever they find it. They break down the food, then the whole colony dies, but not before sending up huge numbers of spores, microscopic seeds that drift in the air until they settle down on a new food source. Molds are very nomadic.

All in the Family

Molds are plantlike organisms called fungi. Mushrooms are too. Fungi don't make food for a living the way green plants do. They eat other things. They eat meat, wood, old shoe leather, cloth, cosmetics, paper, greasy films on walls, wool suits, jet fuel, paint on houses, stone walls, plastic radios, and asphalt roads. Some fungi manage to colonize the surface of the human body.

The fungi family has been breaking down things for millions of years. Fungi are among the first living creatures on earth. They have evolved to live far and wide, and there seems to be a fungus that can thrive on almost every surface.

What's Right About Rot

By now you have probably gotten the impression that the fungus family is a big and successful one. You are right. There are more than 100,000 different kinds of fungi. They are commonly divided into the following basic groups: molds, mildews, blights, rusts, smuts, yeasts, and mushrooms.

Reading this list, you probably get the uneasy feeling that fungi have a bad name. People in general don't have many nice things to say about fungi, with the exception of edible mushrooms. On the other hand, picture a world without rot. All the trees that ever lived would still be standing. The surface of the earth would be stacked high with dead dinosaurs, mastodons, rats, and cats. Oceans would be wall-to wall fish bodies. Compost piles would be miles high. City sewer plants would be too terrible to contemplate. In a week's time we would be drowning in brown bags and cardboard boxes. Beer drinkers would have to switch to milk, and milk would refuse to turn to blue cheese.

If that picture isn't bad enough for you, there is more. The worst part is the fact that all the nutrients for future life and growth would be locked up in brown bags and dead bodies. New life would be impossible. The truth is that fungi do us all a big favor by breaking down things into their elemental parts and returning them to the earth in their basic chemical forms. These chemicals are necessary for life.

That's what's right about rot.

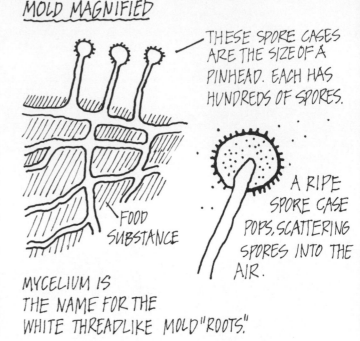

MOLD MAGNIFIED

THESE SPORE CASES ARE THE SIZE OF A PINHEAD. EACH HAS HUNDREDS OF SPORES.

FOOD SUBSTANCE

A RIPE SPORE CASE POPS, SCATTERING SPORES INTO THE AIR.

MYCELIUM IS THE NAME FOR THE WHITE THREADLIKE MOLD "ROOTS."

LEMON DROPS? PERHAPS THEY SHOULD BE CALLED MOLD DROPS. THESE DAYS MOST CITRIC ACID (LEMON FLAVOR) IS MADE FROM FROM A BLACK MOLD KNOWN AS ASPERGILLUS NIGER.

The Fungus Among Us

Fungi will probably show up at your house sooner or later. In fact, you might be able to find a mold or a mildew lurking around your house right now if you know where to look.

Try the refrigerator. The leftover containers in the back often are a microbiologist's delight with colonies of green, gray, white, and even pink molds growing on them.

Look in the breadbox and the fruit bowl for the famous, green penicillin mold. The silver dust on grapes and plums is really a coat of wild yeasts.

Dark, damp closets sometimes produce clothing and shoes with colorful patches of mildews happily growing on their surfaces. Damp cardboard boxes or paper products sometimes have patches of dark, musty-smelling material that are genuine fungi at work.

The pickle jar in the refrigerator, if it has been setting long enough, might be sporting a scum on the surface of the juice that is a living film of yeasts. Water in a vase of flowers, if it hasn't been changed recently, will have a pungent smell that's proof positive that decay organisms are at work on the plant stems.

A dark film on the walls in the kitchen might not be grease from cooking, but a kind of mold that eats grease. Dark spots on the house plants are often an invasion of some blight that finds your indoor greenery irresistible.

In fact, it would be surprising if after a house search, you didn't find a mold or mildew or two.

A Garden from Thin Air

You have looked everywhere and can't find a single fungus at your house. Well, it is possible that your house is very clean, that the refrigerator has been recently defrosted, and that the walls were washed down last week. Never mind. You can grow a mold garden of your own. The seeds or spores for a mold garden are in the air, no matter how clean your house is. If your parents object, tell them it's science.

Here are two ways to grow mold:

1. Set out a slice of boiled potato or a slice of moistened bread on a clean plate. Leave it for an hour.

2. Cover your soon-to-be garden with a plastic bag. Seal the bag.

3. Put the experiment in a warm, dark place.

4. After a few days take a peek. You should have a fine crop of tiny plants. Look at them with your magnifier.

5. Put your garden back for a few more days and grow a wild jungle. Got any ideas about what will happen after that?

SOMETIMES A MOLD COLONY WILL TURN UP IN AN UNEXPECTED PLACE. SAVE IT AND WATCH ITS PROGRESS.

THIS MOLD WAS FOUND ON MY DESK IN A CUP OF OLD TEA:

DAY OF DISCOVERY

3 DAYS LATER

A WEEK OLD

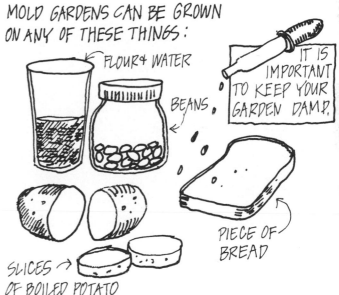

MOLD GARDENS CAN BE GROWN ON ANY OF THESE THINGS:

FLOUR & WATER

BEANS

IT IS IMPORTANT TO KEEP YOUR GARDEN DAMP.

PIECE OF BREAD

SLICES → OF BOILED POTATO

Guide to Microlife

By now you should be convinced that you are never home alone. Your world teems with the unseen. Microlife is everywhere. However, small comes in all sizes. Here is a little guide to life that exists beyond your sight and some notes on relative sizes.

 • AN ENCEPHALITIS VIRUS IS TEENY. IT MEASURES 18 ANGSTROMS (Å). LET'S PRETEND JUST FOR A MINUTE THAT 18 Å IS THE SIZE OF A MARBLE.

 • THEN A FLU VIRUS, 85 Å, WOULD BE THE SIZE OF A TENNIS BALL.

A RICKETTSIA (A KIND OF MICROBE WHICH SOMETIMES LIVES ON TICKS AND CAUSES SPOTTED FEVER) MEASURES 475 Å. IT WOULD BE THE SIZE OF A BASKETBALL.

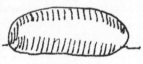 A BACTERIUM, 750 Å, WOULD BE ABOUT THE SIZE OF A GIANT WATERMELON.

 A RED BLOOD CELL, 7500 Å, WOULD BE ABOUT THE LENGTH OF A TAXI CAB.

 A SPIDER MITE, JUST VISIBLE TO THE NAKED EYE, MEASURES 2,500,000 Å AND WOULD BE ABOUT THE LENGTH OF A FREIGHT TRAIN.

Molds in Your Mouth

Do people actually chew up and swallow rotten old molds? That's right, and they pay highly for the privilege. Some of the most expensive cheeses are nothing more than carefully cultured mold gardens growing on milk that has turned solid due to the action of microorganisms. Roquefort or blue cheese is covered with our old friend the penicillin mold. Camembert, Brie, Stilton, and Wensleydale are cheeses that get their special flavors from the molds growing in them. To some people these cheeses taste like old socks. To others they are divine.

Water Drop Magnifier

A single drop of water will act as a magnifier. The curved, clear surface of the drop will bend light in the same way a lens does. It won't do a precision job, and it doesn't magnify a whole lot, but it is cheap to make. All you need is a big nail, a block of wood, and a drop of water.

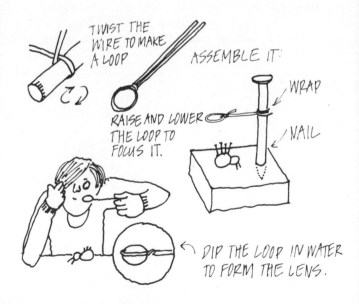

TWIST THE WIRE TO MAKE A LOOP

ASSEMBLE IT:

RAISE AND LOWER THE LOOP TO FOCUS IT.

WRAP

NAIL

← DIP THE LOOP IN WATER TO FORM THE LENS.

The Old Sourdough

There are some people who were named after the microbeasts they carried around with them. The forty-niner gold miners of the gold rush days in California were named for the crock of wild yeasts they toted over the rough hill country. These were the microcreatures that these rough, tough miners used to make their bread and flapjacks.

Sourdough bread wasn't invented by these miners. For centuries people had known that if they left a sugar, water, and flour mixture in the open air, there was a good chance wild things would settle on it. The problem was that all sorts of wild things might turn up, or perhaps not the right ones. When a person did get a colony of wild yeasts he liked, he did his best to keep it alive. The colony would be fed sugar and flour when bread was going to be made. As long as a piece of the original colony was left and it was well fed and protected from freezing, a colony could live for a very long time. A miner kept careful watch on his starter. Sometimes in cold weather he would take it to bed with him to keep it warm.

If it froze, it was death for the microcolony. The miner had to start a new one. On the other hand, a happy, well-fed colony can thrive for years. They sometimes have been kept for generations.

Microsoup

Ever since people discovered the tasty effects of certain molds and yeasts, they have done their best to provide those organisms with happy environments. If you liked growing the bread mold garden, you might enjoy finding out what conditions molds like best.

You will need:
        4 glasses
        2 bouillon cubes
        sugar, salt, vinegar, boiling water

It's a good idea to know what a mold doesn't like so you can discourage the ones you would rather not have around.

1. Dissolve the two bouillon cubes in two glasses of hot water. Let them cool to room temperature.
2. Fill four clean glasses half-full of bouillon.
3. Let the glasses set uncovered for one hour.
4. Add one teaspoon of vinegar to the first.
5. Add one teaspoon of sugar to the second.
6. Add one teaspoon of salt to the third.
7. Add nothing to the fourth.
8. Mark each glass.
9. Seal each in a plastic bag and let all four stand in a warm spot for two days.
10. After two days uncover the glasses and let your nose tell you which glasses have the most mold activity.

Magnifiers: Making Little Large

There are whole other worlds in your house that you have probably never noticed because they're not too noticeable. In fact, some of these worlds are entirely invisible to your eyes. There are tools that will help you break out of the space barriers: lenses bend light to make little things look bigger.

JUST IMAGINE YOURSELF TWICE (2X) YOUR ACTUAL SIZE. OR HOW ABOUT 4X YOUR ACTUAL SIZE? A LITTLE MAGNIFICATION GOES A LONG WAY.

WOW, LOOK AT THOSE TOE NAILS.

THERE ARE TWO BASIC MAGNIFIERS: SIMPLE AND COMPOUND (SUCH AS MICROSCOPES). COMPOUND LENSES GIVE HIGHER MAGNIFICATION, BUT ARE A LOT HARDER TO USE. USE SIMPLE LENSES FOR THE PROJECTS IN THIS BOOK. IF YOU CAN'T FIND ONE CLOSE TO HOME, HERE ARE SOME SEND AWAYS. WRITE FOR THE CURRENT PRICES.

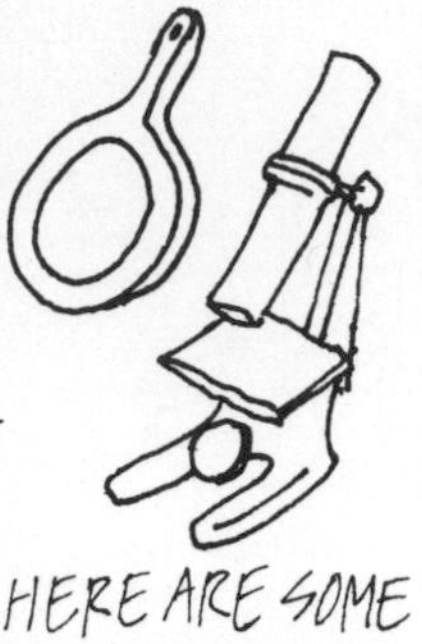

WHAT A LENS CAN DO:

☞ — A FLY LEG (ACTUAL SIZE)

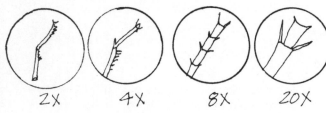

2X   4X   8X   20X

A GOOD SHARP IMAGE IS IMPORTANT. DON'T SETTLE FOR THE FUZZIES. RAISE AND LOWER THE LENS UNTIL THE EDGES OF THE IMAGE ARE SUPERSHARP. IT IS BEST TO USE A QUALITY, LOWER POWERED LENS.

8X GOOD QUALITY PLASTIC LENS. GREAT FOR TABLETOPS. ($4.50 LAWRENCE HALL)

10X QUALITY POCKET LENS. GOOD FOR OUTDOORS. ($5.00 NATURE CO.)

BUG BOXES WITH 4X MAGNIFYING LID. GREAT FOR KEEPING CRAWLERS. (THEY COST ABOUT $4.95 PER DOZEN, BOTH PLACES)

3X, 5X, 8X COMBINATION MAGNIFIER. ($1.00 LAWRENCE HALL)

20X POCKET MICROSCOPE. GOOD FOR LOOKING AT SURFACES. ($15.95 NATURE COMPANY)

DISCOVERY CORNER
LAWRENCE HALL OF SCIENCE
UNIVERSITY OF CALIFORNIA
BERKELEY, CA 94720

NATURE COMPANY
P.O. BOX 7137
1999 EL DORADO
BERKELEY, CA 94707

Sunlight and Green Leaves

There in the middle of the living room rug, in broad daylight, in front of everyone, the fern is photosynthesizing.

That's right, photosynthesizing, a big word that means light (photo) producing (synthesizing). That plant is producing food quietly without any fuss. It needs only a few raw materials: carbon dioxide from the air, water, a few minerals, and sunlight. The product of this process is a simple sugar, which the plant uses immediately or stores for later use in a converted form as starch. Some of the starch is further converted into proteins and oils.

How it accomplishes this magic is something of a mystery. We do know that the green substance called chlorophyll is an important component in this process. It is the same substance that gives a plant its green color. In fact, scavenger plants, such as fungi that live by breaking down green plant bodies, are easy to spot. They have no telltale green color to identify them as food producers.

Plants are the only creatures on earth that have mastered the trick of turning sunlight into food. All animal life depends either directly or indirectly on the food that plants make. All the rest of us creatures are parasites on the green world.

Plant Tattoo

PAPER CLIP

PAPER CUTOUT

Have you ever considered what would happen to a plant that was put on a light starvation diet? You can easily deprive a single leaf of a bit of light for a period of time to get an idea of the results. You will need a paper cutout, a paper clip, and a green plant with a broad leaf. Any outdoor plant leaf will do if you don't have an indoor plant that fits this description.

What's happening? How long does it take to get a reaction? How long does it take to return to normal?

1. Cut out three paper shapes about 2 inches by 2 inches.

2. Clip them to the plant's leaves. Be careful not to damage the plant.

3. Leave one on for a day, the second on for three days, and the third on for a week.

Plant Breath

When you walk into a plant store or a nursery, the atmosphere is different. It smells cool and green and deliciously alive. It's not only your imagination or your love of plants. People who wouldn't give a fig for a ficus can notice the difference. You are moving into an environment that is rich in oxygen. The abundance of this gas that we all love to breathe gives you a special feeling. Oxygen is euphoric. It makes you feel a bit lightheaded and giddy.

It is no wonder you feel good in a greenhouse. Green plants breathe out oxygen. Also they convert carbon dioxide, the stale air you breathe out of your lungs, to oxygen, the gas you need to carry on life. Not a bad trade.

Can you guess why we send plants to people who are sick in bed?

THE CUSTOM OF BRINGING FLOWERS TO A SICK PERSON STARTED AROUND 1775 AFTER PRIESTLEY DISCOVERED PLANTS BREATHE OUT OXYGEN, THE SAME LIFE-GIVING GAS WE BREATHE IN.

Plants as Humidifiers

You can get an idea of how much water a houseplant sends into the air from the surface of its leaves. All you need is a clear plastic bag that is big enough to set the plant in without crushing it and something to tie the bag shut.

1. Set the plant in the bag and close it with the tie.
2. Come back later to see what has happened.

What do you think would become of a plant that is left to grow in a plastic bag? Try it and see.

HMMN... LOOK AT ALL THAT WATER.

DID YOU KNOW THAT A HOUSEPLANT CAN BREATHE OUT 1½ PINTS OF WATER INTO THE AIR EVERY 24 HOURS?

Life Down Under

We tend to think of plants as graceful green things and forget all about the underground life of a plant. Pots are not just a kind of furniture for plants to stick their feet into. Pots are the home of the other half of the green plant, the very important part called the roots.

The upstairs green part is breathing out oxygen, chucking out huge quantities of water into the air, sunning itself while making food, and generally carrying on the work of photosynthesis. Downstairs the hard-working roots have a tough job to do. They search out water and necessary minerals, suck them up, and send them along to the stem.

If you have ever pulled a plant out of its pot, you know that the roots take their job very seriously. If the plant has been living for a long time in the same pot,

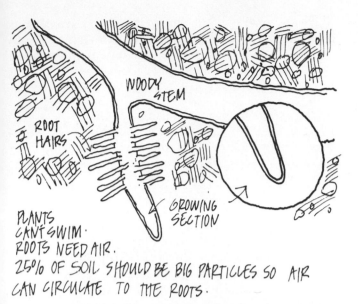

WOODY STEM

ROOT HAIRS

GROWING SECTION

PLANTS CANT SWIM. ROOTS NEED AIR. 25% OF SOIL SHOULD BE BIG PARTICLES SO AIR CAN CIRCULATE TO THE ROOTS.

are the root's lips. All the feeding takes place here. These little hairs wrap themselves around individual bits of soil and suck them dry of water and minerals dissolved in the soil. Hairs live only a short time and are continually being replaced by new ones growing just behind the tip. In this way the plant is constantly seeking out new territory from which to nourish itself.

Keeping Track

Have you ever wondered how much a plant grows in a day or a week?

This method works with a plant that grows in an upright way like a seedling does. Plant a bean or some other seed to satisfy your curiosity.

1. Put the pot indoors next to a window.

2. When the sprout shows its tip, mark it and date it on a strip of paper you have taped next to the plant.

3. When the plant gets a bit bigger, insert a length of broom straw through the tip of the leaf. Mark the plant's progress every day or so.

the whole pot will be choked with roots. There was once a scientist who was so impressed with the roots of a rye plant that he measured them. He found that the roots of a single plant in a little pot (one inch square and two inches deep) would cover about 7,000 square feet.

How do these roots find their way into every nook and cranny inside the pot? They may look like pale delicate threads, but they are strong fellows able to burrow through the toughest soils. The slender root tip seeks out the empty places in the soil. The force of a growing root is only a pound or two, but exerted in needlelike fashion, this pressure is a tremendous force.

The root tip shoves its way through the soil, pushed ahead by the growing cells directly behind the tip, where the root does all of its growing. The thick woody roots of a plant are old sections that are now simply acting as pipelines to the upstairs part of the plant.

Most of the action in the root occurs at the tip and just behind it. If you look closely, you will see that the end of the root is covered with tiny hairs. These hairs

DOES YOUR PLANT GROW ANY FASTER DURING SUNNY SPELLS?

Underside Guide to Leaves

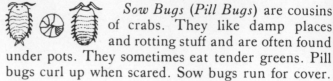

Lurking quietly on the undersides of the leaves of your African violets could be a wild world that you have never considered. There are several species of small animals that are born, eat, sleep, mate, and hatch their young on or about the green life in the pot. The plants in your house might be homes to one or more kinds of these small beasts.

Beasts indeed. If you are an indoor gardener, you will think of these creatures as a horrible menace. On the other hand, you might find them interesting. Creep up and inspect some tiny life under a leaf.

The following list includes some of the animals that you might find living the good life on your indoor plants. It is not a complete list.

Fungus Gnats eat roots. These little flies lay eggs in soil. These hatch into maggots, which munch on plant roots. You might see adults swarm around windows to which they are attracted by the light.

Spider Mites (*Red Spiders*) aren't called mites for nothing. They are very tiny. They look like bits of red dust under the leaves, except this dust has legs—six in the larva stage, eight as adults. They are cousins of spiders and weave loose webs on leaves. You will see their webs if you have a teeming mite population.

Sow Bugs (*Pill Bugs*) are cousins of crabs. They like damp places and rotting stuff and are often found under pots. They sometimes eat tender greens. Pill bugs curl up when scared. Sow bugs run for cover.

Springtails jump by using taillike parts as a spring. They live in soil. You may see their shiny dark bodies on the soil after watering. They chew holes in tender stems and leaves.

White Flies. If you disturb a plant and see flying white dots, you have white flies. Adults flit around the room during the day and live under leaves at night. Their babies look like sesame seeds on the underside of leaves. Adults are covered with a waxy powder, except for their eyes. Like aphids, they secrete "honeydew."

Thrips are tiny slender flealike insects. They will fly when disturbed. Adults are dark; younger ones are orange. They have raspy mouths.

Mealybugs stay pretty still. They grow in clusters under leaves on the stems. You might see mealybug eggs, which are laid in a waxy, white fuzz.

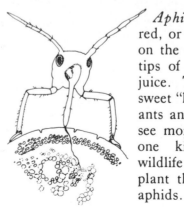

Aphids can be green, pink, red, or black. They are found on the underside and growing tips of leaves, drinking plant juice. They secrete a sticky sweet "honeydew" that attracts ants and molds, so you might see more than one kind of wildlife on a plant that has aphids.

The Dirty Low-Down Life

There could be a couple of billion living, breathing beings happily eating, reproducing, and dying right there in the middle of your living room. In fact, the number might be much higher. Your living room could be teeming with zillions of these beings. They live under the Boston fern or the potted palm or whatever potted indoor greenery lives at your house. Well, not exactly *under* the plant, but in the soil, or more accurately, in the spaces between the bits of soil.

Soil is amazing stuff. It is made of lots of tiny crumbs of rocks. Some are very fine like clay; some are relatively big hunks like grains of sand. Between these tiny pieces are tunnels and pockets that trap water and dead bits of plant. Each crumb of soil has a tight-fitting skin of water and oxides that cling to it. A British scientist once estimated that a single ounce of soil could have a surface area amounting to six acres. That's a lot of nooks and crannies where tiny creatures can hang out. It's a whole other world waiting to be colonized.

And colonized it is. A spoonful of healthy soil from the forest floor is estimated to contain about five billion bacteria, a million tiny animals called protozoa, about twenty million microscopic plants called actinomycetes, and a quarter million fungi and algae. Not to mention the insects, mites, millipedes, worms, spiders, and woodlife. Altogether it's quite a crowd.

The soil snuggled around your potted palm may not contain quite these numbers of small creatures. Often soil that is going to be used indoors for potting is cooked or sterilized in some way. Perhaps you can guess why.

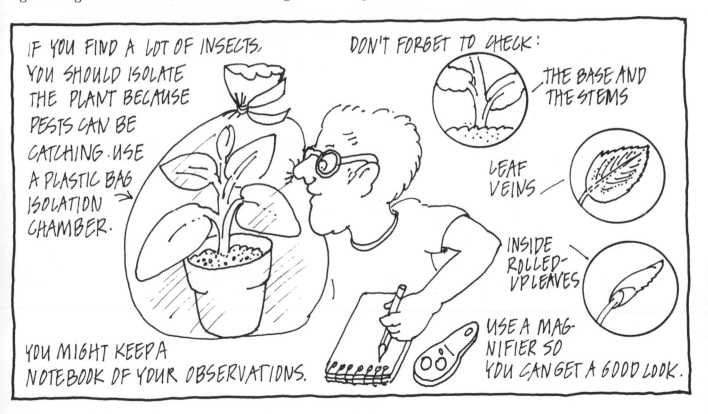

IF YOU FIND A LOT OF INSECTS, YOU SHOULD ISOLATE THE PLANT BECAUSE PESTS CAN BE CATCHING. USE A PLASTIC BAG ISOLATION CHAMBER.

YOU MIGHT KEEP A NOTEBOOK OF YOUR OBSERVATIONS.

DON'T FORGET TO CHECK:

THE BASE AND THE STEMS

LEAF VEINS

INSIDE ROLLED-UP LEAVES

USE A MAGNIFIER SO YOU CAN GET A GOOD LOOK.

Amazing Nematodes

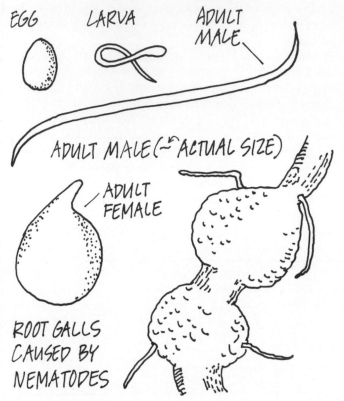

EGG

LARVA

ADULT MALE

ADULT MALE (~ ACTUAL SIZE)

ADULT FEMALE

ROOT GALLS CAUSED BY NEMATODES

Who are these nematode creatures? Have you ever met one? Not unless you are accustomed to crawling around on your hands and knees peering between particles of soil. Nematodes are very small. The largest of them measures less than the size of the period at the end of this sentence. They are tiny eellike creatures that are cousins of the worm.

Despite their tiny size they are animals that come complete with nerves, muscles, and mouths. They are most famous for their mouths. Nematode mouths are designed for piercing the tough skins of other organisms and sucking out their juices. Nematodes apply their efficient mouths to bacteria, protozoa, fungi, and, last but not least, the roots of plants. Not every kind of plant, but ones like gardenias and begonias and about two thousand others in pots, fields, and forests.

The root-rot nematode finds its way to a tasty root by swimming through the soil. It bites the plant root and injects it with a special fluid that causes the plant to grow giant cells, like galls on a tree. These cells grow into giant knots on the roots and encase the nematode. The creature feeds on the giant cells from the inside. Eventually the female lays her eggs, which rest until the conditions are right. These bundles of eggs, or cysts, can stay in the soil for a long time, until a new host root appears in the area. Somehow these larvae get a chemical signal from a nearby root. Scientists are not sure what that signal is. When it comes, the larvae wriggle out of their cyst to attack the new, tasty root.

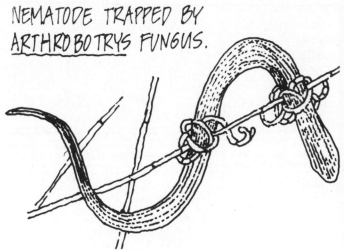

NEMATODE TRAPPED BY ARTHROBOTRYS FUNGUS.

Little Murders

While the nematode drama is going on inside your plant pots, there may be another even more incredible set of events taking place: the attack of the predatory fungus. *Arthrobotrys* is a fungus that normally makes a living digesting organic bits wasting away in the soil.

However, when nematodes are in the area, this fungus becomes a deadly predator. Like the rest of the fungi family, it has a threadlike body called a mycelium. The fungus sends out loops of mycelia, which are sticky and act as snares for unsuspecting nematodes. Caught in these traps, the doomed miniworms are then digested by the plant. The fungus sends the mycelia into the trapped nematode body and drains the life out of it. The fungus then digests its own food tubes and grows off in another direction.

There are more than 50 known kinds of predatory fungi—plants that eat animals.

How to Catch a Nematode

If there are any number of nematodes living in your plant pots and munching on the plant roots, you will notice that the plant is not looking well. (You wouldn't either if someone were nibbling on your roots.) The plant will look yellow and stunted. Eventually it will shrivel up and die.

If you pull up the plant, you will notice that the roots have knots on them. A sure sign of nematodes. Here are instructions to catch one so you can look at it.

You need a soil sample—a couple of teaspoons of soil should be enough—a paper towel, a rubber band, and two paper cups.

1. Cut the bottom out of one of the paper cups.
2. Stretch the paper towel over the bottom of the cutaway cup. Hold the towel in place with the rubber band. Be sure to use the kind of towels that hold together when they get wet.
3. Put the soil sample into the cup on the paper towel.
4. Fill the second cup one-third full of warm water.
5. Set the cup with the soil into the water. Let it set for 24 hours.
6. Remove the soil sample carefully. You should find nematodes in the water of the cup without soil. Look closely, they are very little.

CUT THE BOTTOM OUT OF THIS CUP.
PAPER TOWEL
SOIL
WARM WATER

SLIDE THE SOIL CUP INTO THE WATER CUP.

LET IT SET FOR A DAY. IF YOU ARE LUCKY, YOU WILL FIND NEMATODES IN THE WATER.

POUR THE WATER INTO A GLASS. HOLD IT UP TO THE LIGHT. USE A LENS. NEMATODES LOOK LIKE TINY WIGGLY LINES.

Wall-to-Wall Seeds

If all the seeds in your house suddenly took root and grew into fat green foliage, you would be living in the middle of one very green house. Inside your house there are probably thousands of seeds just waiting for the right conditions to put down roots and get growing.

How did all these seeds get there? If you took a seed survey, you would find that a lot of them traveled in through the front door in a shopping bag. There are also some renegade seeds that snuck in when nobody was looking.

Whether they traveled in on the winds or wrapped up in a watermelon, their aims are the same. The embryonic plants inside those seeds are waiting for some new territory to colonize.

Seeds in Your Socks

How do wild seeds find their way into your house? Some of the fluffy kind rode the wind through an open door or window. There are the clingers and stickers that are designed to hitch rides on passing animals (that includes you and me). Have you ever counted the seeds stuck in your pockets, cuffs, and socks after an outdoor walk? Also, there are the sticky ones—seeds with coats that glue themselves to the mud on your shoes. If you planted your clothes in the garden after such a country stroll, you would be amazed at the number of plants that would sprout from your shirts and pants.

Your parents might be a bit peeved if you planted your clothes. If you're interested in growing some traveling seeds, try this instead.

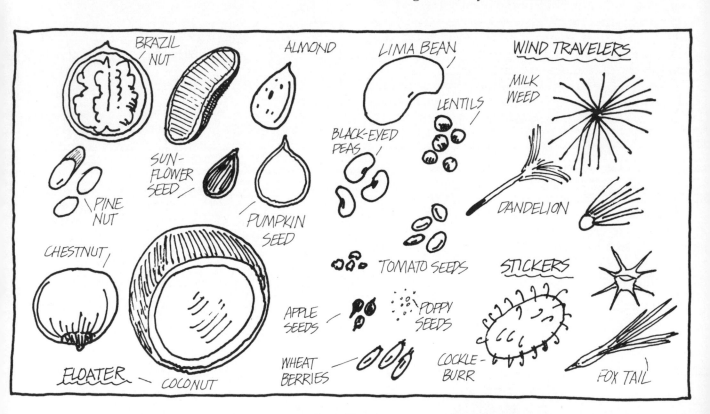

1. Scrape the mud off the bottom of your shoes into some sterilized potting soil. It needs to be sterilized, otherwise you will be growing the seeds that may already be in the soil.

2. Put the mud and soil into a pot and cover it with one-quarter inch of soil. Pack it down. Water well.

3. Cover the pot with a plastic bag. In a week or so you will see what was being walked around on the bottoms of your shoes.

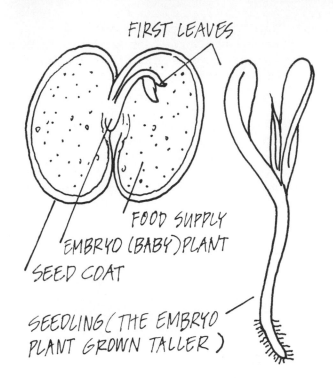

FIRST LEAVES

FOOD SUPPLY
EMBRYO (BABY) PLANT
SEED COAT

SEEDLING (THE EMBRYO PLANT GROWN TALLER)

Inside Seeds

It is easy to see the tiny plant inside a seed if you cut open a large bean or pea. Soak any large seed like a lima or fava bean in water for a day. When the bean gets soft, carefully split it open with a knife. You might need some adult help to do this. You should see a baby plant packed in its own food supply.

Try soaking a bean for a day, another for two, another for three days or up to a week. Split the beans open lengthwise to see how different amounts of time have made changes happen to the plants inside.

Seeds of Survival

A seed could be called a baby plant in a box with its lunch. It's a good description. Packed in along with every plant embryo is a lot of starch and sugar. This food provides nourishment until the young plant starts growing some food-making leaves of its own.

Not only are baby plants able to dine on sugar and starch, so are wild beasts, boll weevils, and birds. Many critters in this world survive by eating the box lunch packed for plant embryos.

Consider your own diet. How many seeds have you had today? None? Think again. How about corn flakes? Corn kernels are seeds. How about crunchy granola? Oats are seeds. So are nuts. Rice Krispies? Breakfast freakies? Both are made from seeds. A piece of toast? Bread is made from wheat flour and that flour is ground from wheat kernels: seeds. (The same would apply to macaroni and spaghetti.) Maybe you had a jelly doughnut—wheat flour again. Besides, a lot of jelly is made from berries, and berries contain seeds. Coffeecake with coconut topping? Coconuts are seeds. Hot chocolate? Chocolate is made from the cocoa bean. And you guessed it, beans are seeds. Coffee too. What about eggs? Not seeds, but did you cook them in margarine? Margarine is made of oil pressed from, right you are, seeds.

That's just breakfast. It's safe to say that seeds are not just for the birds. They are a large part of your diet. In some spots in the world they are the main part. Seeds mean survival for the plant kingdom, and for many species of the animal world.

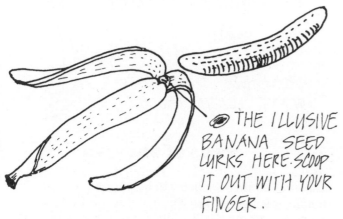

THE ILLUSIVE BANANA SEED LURKS HERE. SCOOP IT OUT WITH YOUR FINGER.

Kitchen Seed Survey

Have you ever seen a banana seed? No, it's not those little dots that appear when you slice one crosswise. Most people have never seen a banana seed, but most people have never looked.

How many kinds of seeds have you seen in your kitchen? Half a dozen? A dozen? More? How many do you think you could find right now? Why don't you go look. Seeds come in a lot of interesting shapes and an amazing number of sizes. And they are definitely worth looking at. While you're out there, try to figure out where the banana puts its seeds.

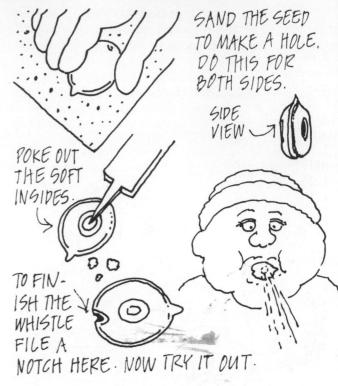

SAND THE SEED TO MAKE A HOLE. DO THIS FOR BOTH SIDES.

SIDE VIEW →

POKE OUT THE SOFT INSIDES.

TO FINISH THE WHISTLE FILE A NOTCH HERE. NOW TRY IT OUT.

Seed Whistle

You can make a whistle out of a seed like the one that comes out of an apricot. You will need some sandpaper, a jackknife or a file, and some elbow grease.

1. Rub the side of the pit on a piece of sandpaper. Keep rubbing until you make a hole in the side of the pit.

2. Now make a hole on the other side by sanding it.

3. File or cut a notch in one end.

4. Poke out the seed inside with a nail or the tip of the file.

To whistle, put the pit next to your teeth. Hold it in place with your lips and blow. Try experimenting with different size holes.

Seed Ring

You can make a ring to wear on your finger or for a friend's finger. You need a seed from a peach or a nectarine.

1. Sand a hole in one side and then in the other. This is easiest if you use rough sandpaper wrapped around a block. Rub the pit against the flat surface.

2. Sand until you can see the seed inside. The hard crinkly part is just the outer shell.

3. Poke out the seed.

4. You can fit the ring. The more you rub, the bigger the hole. Remember to sand both sides equally.

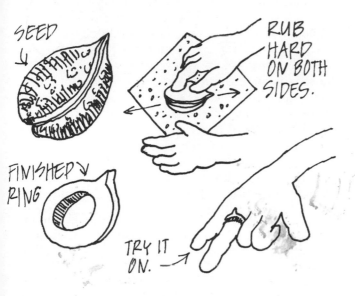

SEED

RUB HARD ON BOTH SIDES.

FINISHED RING

TRY IT ON.

Seed Power

Water is the magic compound that sets the dormant seed into action. Soak some seeds and watch the changes take place.

1. Put some beans into a jar and fill the jar with water.

2. Let set for a couple of hours.

3. Carefully remove the top.

These swollen seeds are ready to grow. Or if you can be so heartless, you can turn them into a tasty baked bean supper. The truth is that here on earth one species generally survives by eating another. That goes for vegetarians too.

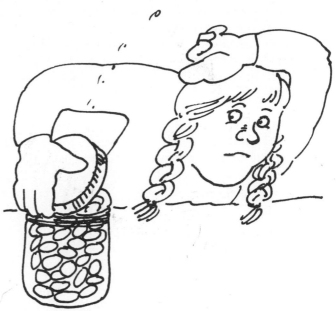

Send Away: Cactus Seeds

Most all plants make seeds of some kind. That goes for cactuses too. You can send away for your very own cactus growing kit. It comes complete with about 50 seeds, soil, and directions on what to do, all contained in a plastic egg. It is an interesting and fun way to grow your own desert on a windowsill. Just add water and wait for the cactus sprouts.

The kits are handpacked and cost $1.25. They are available from the friendly folks at:

K & L Cactus and Succulent Nursery
12712 Stockton Boulevard
Galt, California 95632

The Everyday Edible Bulb

Onions are bulbs. When they are removed from cold storage and set out at room temperature, they start coming to life. They send out shiny, new shoots at the top end. If you put the onion in water, it will send out delicate, white roots at the other end. Pick out one at the supermarket or from the pantry, one that looks healthy and happy and is showing signs of life. Set it in some water and watch it grow.

1. Pick an onion with some green shoots showing at the top.

2. Find a jar that lets the bulb rest in the opening.

3. Pour water into the jar so that it just touches the roots. If the bulb is covered with water, it will spoil.

4. Set the bulb in a window and watch it grow.

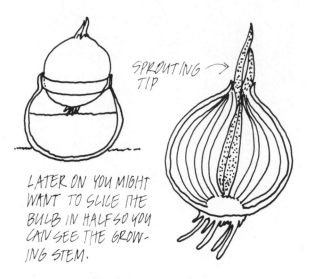

SPROUTING TIP →

LATER ON YOU MIGHT WANT TO SLICE THE BULB IN HALF SO YOU CAN SEE THE GROWING STEM.

Inside a Bulb

A bulb is actually a very short stem that is wrapped up in a bunch of fat, fleshy leaves. These leaves are special. They are where the food is stored in the plant.

Are you interested in having a look at the inside of a bulb? Pick one with some shoots and slice it in half.

It's Alive

You reach into the cupboard to pull out a potato and you grab a handful of long, pale tendrils. The potatoes have turned themselves into a sackful of scary-looking creatures from outer space. Potatoes are not the only vegetable that will transform themselves if left alone. Onions will sprout bright green tops. Turnips and rutabagas will leaf out with curly green topknots. How do they do this?

Potatoes, onions, turnips, and rutabagas are actually packages of stored food. This food has been stored by the plant for its next growing season. (So farming is the cultivation of this food in plants.) Just because a potato was bought at the market doesn't mean that it isn't alive. It is ready to spring into life, given the right conditions. At the proper temperature the potato will start to convert the food stored inside into sprouts and roots. The potato is actually digesting itself. That's why a potato with long sprouts will look shrunken. A lot of food energy inside has been converted into the growing parts of the plant you see on the outside.

This potato tuber is programmed to keep growing until it can put down roots and send up green leaves to make more food. It is looking for soil and sun. It doesn't know that it is captive in your cupboard.

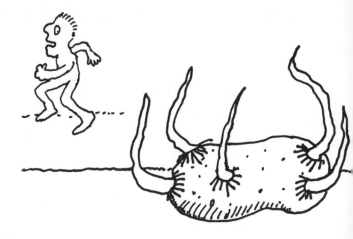

Root Cellar

Warm temperatures and light are the signals for vegetables to get growing. That is why those dull, brown potatoes suddenly spring to life when you bring them home. At the store they are kept very cool. Behind those doors marked "Employees Only" are the cold, dark places where vegetables rest before they are brought to the display counter so you can buy them.

Of course, you don't meet the potato until it gets to the vegetable counter. Then you wheel it past the checker for the trip home. If you look at this trip from the tuber's point of view, suddenly it is spring. That's the signal for it to get growing. Within a few weeks your tuber will be a mass of sprouts. Unless you place your potatoes under cold storage (the tuber's winter), they will have digested themselves before you have a chance to do so.

3
Mountains in the House

Part 3
Mountains in the House

Indoor Geology

Have you ever thought about the mountain parts in your house? Not the occasional pebble you pick up in your shoe, but the rocks that hold your house together? Or the minerals that you sprinkle on your dinner? Or the rocks that you use to brush your teeth? Or those you use to scour the bathtub and the rocks that you walk on? Or the rocks that heat your house? Or the rocks that line your bathtub? Or the rocks that you dust on yourself when you get out of the bath? Or the rocks you use for writing? The list could go on and on.

There are enough rocks in an ordinary house to keep an indoor geologist busy for quite a while. Maybe it's time you found out about them.

The Armchair Rock Hound

You can start your own rock collection with samples picked up from around your house. There is a surprising number of rocks and minerals that you can study without ever going outdoors. One nice

thing about indoor geology is that positive identification of your specimens is easy. Unlike the outdoor geologist who has to play guessing games with every rock he finds, you will know just where to find a sample of halite. You won't make a mistake; it will be clearly marked in the kitchen as table salt.

An indoor geologist can find all the equipment and samples needed right around the house. An empty egg carton is a perfect place to keep your samples. Put a different kind in each space.

A hammer is a handy piece of equipment for breaking big pieces into sample sizes. Be sure to wear goggles when breaking samples. Flying fragments can be dangerous.

Magnifiers are useful for looking up close. A notebook is handy for keeping any discoveries you might make about your rocks. Keep a separate page for each specimen.

Corners of plastic bags make good pouches for some of your powdery samples.

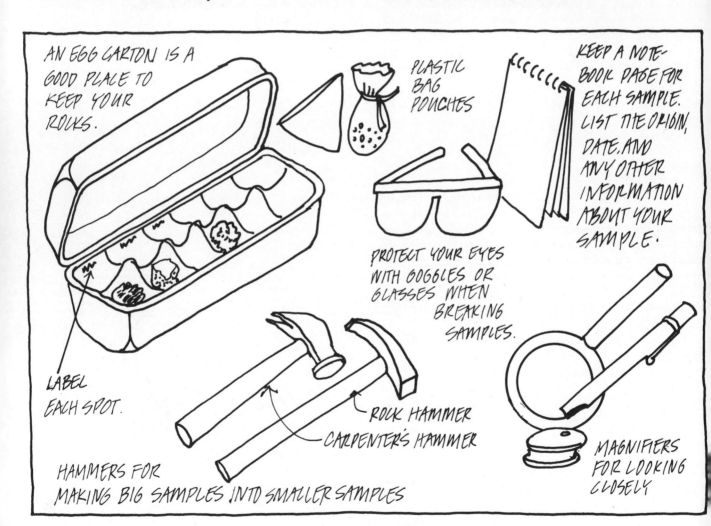

AN EGG CARTON IS A GOOD PLACE TO KEEP YOUR ROCKS.

PLASTIC BAG POUCHES

KEEP A NOTEBOOK PAGE FOR EACH SAMPLE. LIST THE ORIGIN, DATE, AND ANY OTHER INFORMATION ABOUT YOUR SAMPLE.

PROTECT YOUR EYES WITH GOGGLES OR GLASSES WHEN BREAKING SAMPLES.

LABEL EACH SPOT.

ROCK HAMMER
CARPENTER'S HAMMER

MAGNIFIERS FOR LOOKING CLOSELY

HAMMERS FOR MAKING BIG SAMPLES INTO SMALLER SAMPLES

Guide to Indoor Rocks

INSIDE VOLCANO FROTH

BATHTUB PUMICE STONES

Pumice. You will find this rock around bathtubs. It is generally a gray stone that has a rough texture with lots of holes. Its texture makes it a perfect tool for rubbing off dead skin. Pumice stone is actually volcano froth. Look at it closely and you will see it is full of holes. It was blown full of holes by steam escaping from the cooling lava. Because all the holes are filled with trapped air, pumice will float on water. It is sometimes found in toothpaste and other sanding substances.

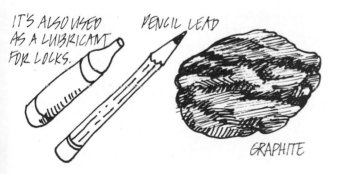

IT'S ALSO USED AS A LUBRICANT FOR LOCKS.

PENCIL LEAD

GRAPHITE

Graphite. You will find thin lines of graphite scrawled across pages. Deposits of it run in thin veins within wooden jackets in desk drawers. Graphite is the lead of pencils. Actually, lead is an old-fashioned term. People used to write with long thin pieces of lead, another soft mineral. The word lead has stuck

to pencils, although a lead pencil is hard to find today. Graphite is one of the softest minerals. It has a metallic luster and a greasy feel. There are three mines in America where these flaky graphite crystals are found. A lot is imported from other countries.

WET CLAY

FIRED, IT BECOMES LIKE ROCK.

IT CAN BE DELICATE OR ROUGH.

Clay. You may have some clay around your house if someone who lives there is a potter. It is quite possible that the dirt under your house is clay. Many soils are clay soils. Most likely if you find clay in the house, it will be in its cooked form: pottery. Clay is rock that has taken a beating. It is composed of tiny particles of rocks that have been broken down into microscopic bits. These stick together when they are wet. Clay deposits form on lake bottoms or places where muddy water settles.

Pottery Rocks. You will have no trouble identifying this stuff. It's a very common man-made rock, made by cooking (firing) clay at high temperatures. The firing causes some of the particles in the clay to melt together to form a hard, brittle type of stone. If you are an observant indoor geologist, you will notice all pottery is not alike. Some is rough and red. Some is fine, white, and glasslike. Don't be fooled by the outside coat of glaze. Take the hammer to a few samples so you can get a look at the inside. You will find that the higher the firing temperature of the clay, the smoother the texture. This is because more of the particles have melted together. Tap it with your fingernail. Some samples thunk. Some clink. Some have a musical ring. More air spaces mean less music.

P.S. Be sure you have permission before you use your hammer on any pottery rocks.

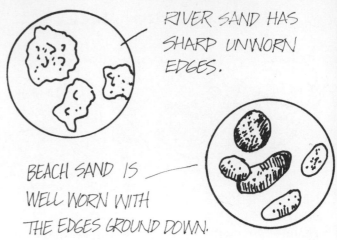

RIVER SAND HAS SHARP UNWORN EDGES.

BEACH SAND IS WELL WORN WITH THE EDGES GROUND DOWN.

Earthenware. This type of pottery is rough, red, and porous (lots of holes). It is often used to make red-colored flower pots.

Stoneware. This nonporous pottery is opaque and often gray. It may be glazed or not.

Porcelain. Glasslike, smooth, fine china. Pure bone-white color (no impurities). Thin pieces will let the light shine through.

Bricks. A mixture of sand and clay that is fired. Very porous.

Sand. Look for it in your pants cuffs, the cat box, the flower pots, and the big ashtrays in office buildings. Actually, sand isn't a type of rock. It is simply broken-down pieces of bigger rocks. Wind and water are the sandmakers. If you look at a handful of sand, you will often see shiny, clear flecks. These are tough little quartz crystals that have broken away from bigger rocks. You can tell whether your sand is beach sand or river sand by looking closely with a magnifying glass. Beach sand is smoother, having been worn away by the action of the waves.

Chalk. You can find sticks of this material not far from a blackboard. Chalk is made of once living creatures called foraminifers. Foraminifers are microscopic marine animals. Their shelly remains, which are made of a mineral called calcium carbonate, settle to the bottom of shallow seas and oceans where they collect in great piles. Chalk deposits are the graveyards of these tiny creatures. Sometimes they collect in deposits many feet thick. The white cliffs of Dover are such a chalk graveyard.

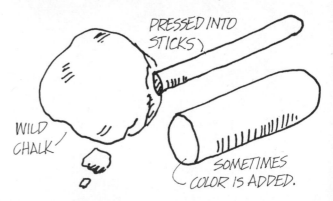

PRESSED INTO STICKS

WILD CHALK!

SOMETIMES COLOR IS ADDED.

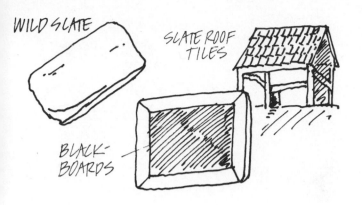

WILD SLATE

SLATE ROOF TILES

BLACK-BOARDS

Slate. In the old days all blackboards were pieces of slate. You may have heard someone call them slates. Slate is a dark gray stone that breaks naturally into thin plates. A slice of it makes a good surface to write on. Sometimes slices of slate were used for roofing tiles. If you can get your hands on a piece of slate and get it wet, you will notice that this shiny, hard rock smells like mud. That's because it used to be mud. It was laid down by the movement of water. Later it was buried and squeezed to a hardened mass, and it still breaks along the layers in which it was laid down.

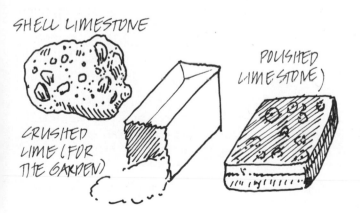

SHELL LIMESTONE

POLISHED LIMESTONE)

CRUSHED LIME (FOR THE GARDEN)

Limestone. Limestone is used on the faces of important buildings such as banks and courthouses. It is also found on old-fashioned soda fountains and on tabletops. It comes in a variety of colors and textures. Sometimes you can see the fossil remains of the marine animals from which it is made. Other creatures, in addition to foraminifers, produce a protective layer of calcium carbonate. Eggshells, clam shells, and corals are made of this material. Limestone, like chalk, is the accumulation of the bodies of these larger creatures.

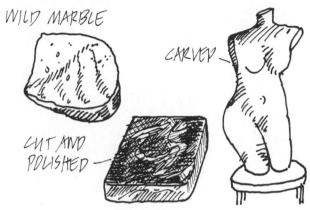

WILD MARBLE

CARVED

CUT AND POLISHED

Marble. You will find that marble is used in the same way as ornamental limestones. The very rarest, pure white marble has always been a favorite of sculptors who work in stone. Michelangelo's famous statue David is carved from marble. It is 16 feet high. You can imagine how many small marine bodies settled down to create that chunk of marble. What's the difference between limestone and marble? A magnifying glass will show you. Marble has tiny flecks of crystal materials that catch the light. Heat and pressure have caused those crystals to form.

Lime. Unless you are a gardener you won't have this around the house in pure form. It is a white, powdery substance that sucks up water and burns the skin. Why on earth would you want something like that? It is used in mortar for sticking bricks together, and it's the basic ingredient for plaster walls and cement driveways. Tom Sawyer couldn't have

69

whitewashed his famous fence without it. Lime is made by pounding limestone into powder then baking it to drive off the water. Later, when water is added again, the lime has the happy ability to stick to things, as in the case of mortar — more magic from the crushed bodies of long dead marine creatures. If you're curious about what it does in the garden, lime is a basic material that works well for neutralizing acid soils.

MORTAR

MORTAR MAGNIFIED (YOU CAN SEE THE SAND STUCK TO-GETHER WITH LIME)

FIND IT STUCK BETWEEN BRICKS.

CONCRETE ROCK,

CONCRETE SIDEWALK

Mortar, Concrete, Plaster. When you break them open, you will notice that they all have different textures. That is because different ingredients are added to the limestone base when making them. Concrete has sand and gravel to make it a stronger stone. If you look, you will see what has been added to plaster and mortar.

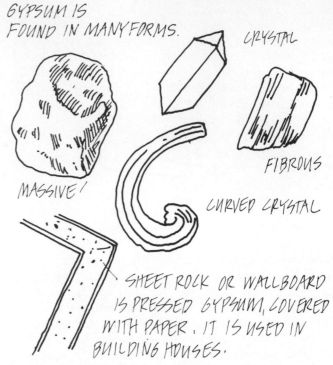

GYPSUM IS FOUND IN MANY FORMS.

CRYSTAL

FIBROUS

MASSIVE

CURVED CRYSTAL

SHEET ROCK OR WALLBOARD IS PRESSED GYPSUM, COVERED WITH PAPER. IT IS USED IN BUILDING HOUSES.

Gypsum. The truth is that most blackboard chalk is not chalk at all, but gypsum. Gypsum is a naturally occurring mineral that is thought to be a sediment left by the drying of seas. In many places deposits of this mineral have been left that are many feet thick. It is also used in making plaster and wallboard for houses.

Plaster of Paris. You might have some of this around the house. If you have a broken bone, it is the white rock that is wrapped around your break. Plaster of Paris is gypsum that has been baked and ground into a fine powder. When water is added to this powder, the mineral recrystallizes into its gypsum form, making a soft, white stone. A lot of heat is released when this happens. Get some plaster of Paris and try casting something with it. In case you're curious, it's called plaster of Paris because it was first mined near Paris a couple of centuries ago.

Talc. Look for this rock in the bathroom. It is in a container under a fluffy powderpuff or in a tall container with holes on the top. It is also known as talcum powder, baby powder, or afterbath dusting powder. Sometimes you might find a cake of it in a sewing box under the name tailor's chalk. These are all the same finely ground, supersoft rock. Talc is at the bottom of the hardness scale. It is found in the wild in many states. By the time it gets to the bathroom it has been ground and purified to a white, greasy-feeling powder that people like to fluff on their skin after a bath. Talc acts as a lubricant. It also absorbs water on your skin.

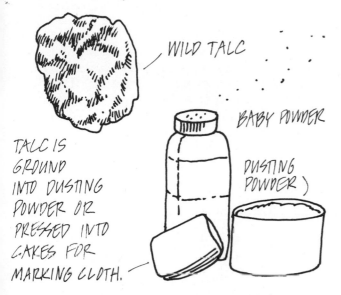

WILD TALC

BABY POWDER

DUSTING POWDER

TALC IS GROUND INTO DUSTING POWDER OR PRESSED INTO CAKES FOR MARKING CLOTH.

Garnets. You probably think you can't afford garnets for your rock collection. Think again. You might already have some garnets out in the garage. All garnets are not the clear, red stones that you have to buy from the jeweler. Most garnets are used for more practical purposes such as making sandpaper. If you don't have any garnet paper in your garage, you can buy a sheet at the hardware store for less than a dime. Take it home and look at it with your magnifier. You will see that the surface is covered with rough bits of rock.

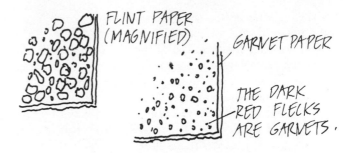

FLINT PAPER (MAGNIFIED)

GARNET PAPER

THE DARK RED FLECKS ARE GARNETS.

Garnets range in color from brown to deep red and are quite hard (7 on a scale of 1 to 10). Crushed, they are quite useful for grinding things down.

P.S. While you are at the hardware store, have a look at the other sandpapers. You will find an exotic selection: silicon carbide, aluminum oxide, flint. Look at them with your pocket magnifier.

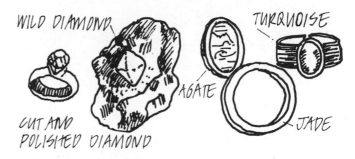

WILD DIAMOND

TURQUOISE

AGATE

CUT AND POLISHED DIAMOND

JADE

Jewel Box Rocks. There are household rocks that you won't be able to get samples of, rocks like diamonds, rubies, jade, and turquoise. Actually, geologists call these rocks by another name: minerals. Or, more exactly, gemstone minerals. These are the beauties of the rock world. They are prized for their color, crystal clearness, and strength.

What's the difference between a rock and a mineral? It's rather like the difference between an ice cube and a chocolate chip cookie. One is made of a pure substance while the other is a hodgepodge of ingredients. Rocks are flecked and specked with all kinds of things. They are the mongrels of the geology world. They make up most of the earth's crust. Minerals are pure elements or compounds and are a rare occurrence, one reason they are so highly prized. You won't get a diamond ring for your collection, but there is another place to look for one. The needle on the record player may have a point that is a piece of a diamond. You are not going to be dazzled by this particular diamond since it is quite small and not much to look at. However, you could marvel at the toughness of this tiny tip that will cover miles and miles of record grooves in its lifetime. Diamonds are chosen for this job because they are the hardest of all rocks. Don't wait too long before asking for the old needle. Even diamonds wear away eventually.

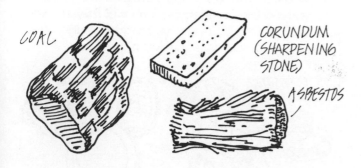

COAL

CORUNDUM (SHARPENING STONE)

ASBESTOS

More Rocks. There is no need to stop here because there are other rocks not on this list. There are rocks and minerals such as borax, coal, corundum (the kind of stone used for sharpening knives), halite (also known as table salt), asbestos, and glass (a man-made crystal). You can find out more about them by looking in the encyclopedia.

How to Look at Rocks

All rocks are not alike.

Some are soft like chalk. Some are hard like diamonds. Some are stringy. Some are flaky. Some float. Some feel greasy. Some are rough. Some shatter. Some are tough. Rocks vary according to their basic ingredients (elements) and how they were formed. They come in an amazing variety.

Often to get a sample rock for your collection you will have to break it down with your hammer. Notice that rocks don't break alike. Some shatter, leaving behind sharp pointy edges. Others flake or even break off, leaving behind nice smooth surfaces. Geologists pay attention to how rocks break. It helps identify them.

FLAKY   SMOOTH   SHARP

GRAINY

Once your sample is broken is a perfect time to look inside. Move your rock and magnifier to a bright light. Look closely at your sample. You may find tiny flakes or thousands of crystals. Take your time looking closer. It will be worth your while.

The insides of rocks will surprise you. White powders may turn out to be thousands of crystals. Pumice will look like a mountain with millions of caves. Sometimes there are stringy pieces. A broken brick will reveal sand and smooth clay.

MUD DAUBERS ARE WASPS. THE FEMALE MAKES MUD NESTS THAT HAVE TUBES IN WHICH SHE PUTS HER EGGS AND A PARALYZED SPIDER TO SERVE AS FOOD WHEN THE YOUNG HATCH. THEY ARE COMMON AROUND BARNS, HOUSES, AND SHEDS, UNDER THE EAVES WHEREVER THERE IS MUD AND A GOOD SUPPLY OF SPIDERS.

Plaster of Paris Feet

You can have your very own clodhoppers cast in plaster. Plaster of Paris is interesting stuff to use. It is a white powder that can be converted to rock by adding water then allowing it to dry. Heat is created in the process. In its liquid state you can shape it into all sorts of things.

Buy your plaster of Paris at the building supply or hardware store. It's pretty cheap in five-pound bags. You will need at least that much for your plaster feet.

You will need an old shoe box, some damp sand, a sheet of plastic, and plaster of Paris.

PUT YOUR FOOT DOWN TO MAKE A GOOD IMPRESSION.

PLASTIC LINER

DAMP SAND

POUR LIQUID PLASTER INTO THE PRINT.

YOUR SIZE SHOE BOX

LET IT DRY. THEN REMOVE THE FOOT AND SAND IT OFF.

1. Line the box with the sheet of plastic.
2. Pour in the damp sand. If you work indoors, put some newspaper under the box.
3. Stand in the sand to make a footprint. You might have to do this a couple of times to get a deep, clear print.

4. To mix up the plaster of Paris pour the plaster into a big can and add water, a little at a time, until the plaster looks like thick cream. Stir it while you do this.
5. Pour the plaster into the footprint.
6. Let it dry for a couple of hours.
7. Take it out. Brush off the sand. Smooth the foot into shape with some sandpaper.
8. Figure out something to do with it.

Bubbles from Boulders

Here is an acid test that geologists use to find out if a rock is a carbonate. Calcium carbonate is the substance that forms the shells of the animals that we talked about earlier. Plunk a sample of a suspected carbonate in an acid. If it is, in fact, a carbonate, carbon dioxide gas will bubble forth.

To test for carbonates you will need some vinegar (distilled white vinegar is the easiest to see through); a tall, narrow glass; and some samples (you might try blackboard chalk, plaster of Paris, marble, baking soda, crushed eggshells or seashells, talc, or scouring powder).

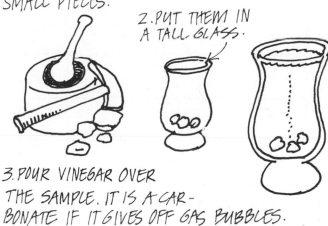

1. BREAK THE SAMPLE INTO SMALL PIECES.

2. PUT THEM IN A TALL GLASS.

3. POUR VINEGAR OVER THE SAMPLE. IT IS A CARBONATE IF IT GIVES OFF GAS BUBBLES.

Hard as a Rock

All rocks are not of the same hardness. Some rocks are so soft you can break them apart with your bare hands. Some are so hard they are used for cutting through the toughest materials known. In fact, the only way that a diamond can be cut and polished is to do so with another diamond. Hardness is often an important clue in identifying a mystery stone. Geologists use a 1-to-10 system called Mohs' scale (Mohs rhymes with toes) to estimate rock hardness. It works like this: A mineral will scratch anything that is as hard or softer than itself. Scratch-test your samples.

The illustration below combines Mohs' scale with a list of some around-the-house items that are about equal to the mineral hardness scale. You might want to collect these items for a hardness kit you can carry around whenever you think you might meet up with some tough rocks.

HARDNESS	MINERAL	SCRATCHER (THESE HOUSEHOLD ITEMS WILL WORK AS TOOLS FOR TESTING HARDNESS.)
1	TALC	SOFT PENCIL LEAD
2	GYPSUM	BLACKBOARD CHALK FINGERNAIL (2.5?)
3	CALCITE	COPPER PENNY
4	FLUORITE	BRASS
5	APATITE	CARPENTER'S NAIL
6	ORTHOCLASE	STEEL FILE
7	QUARTZ	FLINT SANDPAPER
8	TOPAZ	(NONE)
9	CORUNDUM	EMERY SANDPAPER
10	DIAMOND	CARBORUNDUM SANDPAPER (9½)

SOFT →

← HARD

SCRATCH A SAMPLE WITH YOUR FINGERNAIL.

LEAVES A MARK?

TRY SOMETHING HARDER. NO MARK? YOUR SAMPLE IS 2½ ON MOHS' SCALE.

GEOLOGISTS REMEMBER THE HARDNESS ORDER WITH THIS CATCHY SENTENCE:"THE GIRLS CAN FLIRT AND OTHER QUEER THINGS CAN DO." THE FIRST LETTER REPRESENTS T FOR TALC, G FOR...

Hard as Which Rock?

Try scratching your sample rocks with your fingernail. This is a handy place to start. No scratches? Then try something harder, like a nail file. Still no scratches? Try something still harder, such as flint paper. Ah ha, scratches. Will something softer work? A steel file leaves scratches also? Then your sample has a hardness of 6 on Mohs' scale.

Geologists remember the hardness order of rocks with this catchy phrase: "The girls can flirt and other queer things can do." The first letter of each word in the phrase is the first letter of talc, gypsum, calcite, and so on.

Send Away:
The Magic Crystal

Borax is a handy mineral to have. In fact, you may have some around your house right now. It is sometimes used in the washing machine to help clean clothes. The ancient dried-up lake known as Death Valley is a famous source of borax. If you would like to know more about borax, how it was mined, and how it was pulled out of this hot spot by big teams of mules, send for the booklet "The Magic Crystal." It also tells some other uses for this around-the-house mineral. It is free from:

United States Borax and Chemical Company
3075 Wilshire Boulevard
Los Angeles, California 90010

Rock Beauties

It sets on everybody's table, you sprinkle it on your food, and you couldn't live without it. If you are like most people, you have never noticed what it really looks like up close. Unless you have taken a look at it with a good magnifying glass, you would never know that this ho-hum white powder is actually a miniature mountain of wildly beautiful, natural crystals.

Salt isn't the only everyday, around-the-house substance that shapes itself into beautiful, symmetrical shapes. Get out your magnifier and get a load of the sugar bowl. The stuff that you sprinkle on your corn flakes comes in a different but equally fascinating crystal shape. There is old boring borax, the stuff some people pour into the wash. There are mothballs and epsom salts. Grab your best magnifier (a pocket microscope is best) and have a look.

Wild Crystals

The crystals around your house don't all come out of bags or boxes. You are apt to run across some wild crystals growing in undisturbed corners of your house at this very moment.

Check the freezer. If you don't have a newfangled, frostfree refrigerator, you are likely to find a layer of ice crystals lining the freezer walls. Have you scrutinized the pancake syrup lately? No? Well, have a look. You might see wild crystals growing on the inside surface, especially if the lid is loose. The same goes for the honey pot.

What causes ordinary, around-the-house substances to turn themselves into hard, orderly rocks? The easy answer is evaporation. Certain liquids and gases, when they cool and lose water, form crystals. This happens in the earth's crust and it happens in your kitchen.

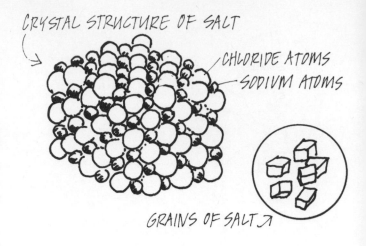

CRYSTAL STRUCTURE OF SALT

CHLORIDE ATOMS
SODIUM ATOMS

GRAINS OF SALT ↗

A Crystal Is

When the molecules of a material are all the same shape, they can fit together in a nice, orderly package. This package is called a crystal. Not all substances can become crystals because their molecules have different shapes and will not fit together neatly. These substances are plain, everyday solids.

Sound confusing? Pretend that molecules are wooden building blocks. Suppose all the molecules of one substance are cubes. They will pack together smoothly, no matter how many cubes you add. Now suppose that the molecules of another substance are building blocks shaped like bananas. No matter how hard you try, you can't fit them together neatly. All you can do is to bunch them together in a mixed-up lump.

The special qualities of a crystal are the result of the way its molecules pack together. Each crystal has a characteristic shape. (How many ways can you squeeze a handful of marbles or wooden cubes together?) This orderly shape lets light through, giving crystals their clear appearance. If you glued your marbles or wooden cubes together and hit them, chances are they would break along the joints or seams. This is why crystals fracture along even lines.

SPREAD A TINY PINCH OF CRYSTALS ON A DARK BACKGROUND.

SALT CRYSTALS ARE CUBES.

EPSOM SALTS ARE NEEDLE-SHAPED.

YOU CAN MAKE CRYSTALS BY LETTING A FEW DROPS OF LIQUID MOUTHWASH EVAPORATE ON A GLASS. ALSO TRY BATH SALTS, ASPIRIN, AND ALUM.

Crystals on a Plate

Here is another way to grow some crystals. This way is faster and you can get long, flat, needle-shaped crystals. You can watch the atoms unpack as they melt from the solid to the liquid state. You need a sheet of glass, some water, and a freezer.

1. Pour the water onto the sheet of glass.
2. Put it in the freezer.
3. Remove it when it is frozen and look at it. The crystals won't last long out of the freezer.

Rocks from Liquids

Do you want to try a disappearing act? You can perform a bit of crystal magic right in your kitchen.

To make salt crystals:

1. Dissolve one teaspoon of salt in one cup of water.

2. Heat the mixture over a low flame to evaporate the water. What is left?

3. Look at the salt crystals under a microscope. What shape are the crystals?

What conditions make bigger crystals?

If you boiled some sea water, what do you think you would have left in the pan?

You can try this evaporation-by-boiling method with any household crystals, especially the ones in powdered form, which will produce bigger crystals.

FREEZE SOME WATER ON A SHEET OF GLASS.

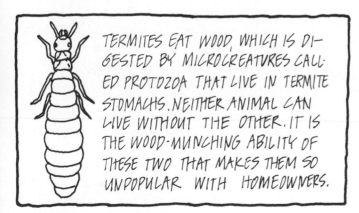

TERMITES EAT WOOD, WHICH IS DIGESTED BY MICROCREATURES CALLED PROTOZOA THAT LIVE IN TERMITE STOMACHS. NEITHER ANIMAL CAN LIVE WITHOUT THE OTHER. IT IS THE WOOD-MUNCHING ABILITY OF THESE TWO THAT MAKES THEM SO UNPOPULAR WITH HOMEOWNERS.

Mysterious Stuff Dust

Some time when the conditions are just right indoors, you will see a single beam of light coming in through a window, slashing across the room. If you are in the right position, you will notice that you are not alone. There are thousands, no millions, of tiny particles dancing around in the air. Every house has it. Even if the windows and doors are shut tight, it will collect on the surfaces of things. It's the constant wiping and dusting that keeps furniture from being buried under thick layers of dust.

What is dust and where does it come from? A simple question. Just try to find a simple answer. A lot of people will tell you that it is dirt. Don't take dirt for an answer. There is no way that those heavy chunks of grit from the bottoms of your shoes are going to float around in the air as dust. Take a close look and you'll find that the dirt on the floor is different from the dust on the piano. The truth is that dust is something of a mystery.

Dust Detective

HOW TO COLLECT DUST

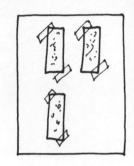

1. PRESS A PIECE OF CELLO-PHANE TAPE INTO A DUSTY SPOT.

2. PULL IT UP AND TAPE IT FACE UP ON A PAPER.

NOW ITS TIME TO GET OUT THE MAGNIFIER TO SEE WHAT YOU PICKED UP. HERE'S WHAT YOU MAY FIND:

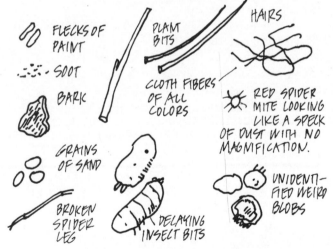

FLECKS OF PAINT

SOOT

BARK

GRAINS OF SAND

BROKEN SPIDER LEG

PLANT BITS

CLOTH FIBERS OF ALL COLORS

DECAYING INSECT BITS

HAIRS

RED SPIDER MITE LOOKING LIKE A SPECK OF DUST WITH NO MAGNIFICATION.

UNIDENTI-FIED WEIRD BLOBS

Find out for yourself where this mysterious stuff comes from. The best place to start is with a few samples and a magnifying glass or a pocket microscope. Once you have a good idea of what it is, it should be easy figuring out where it comes from. You can collect it from surfaces on strips of scotch tape.

You can sometimes find big clumps of it collecting in out of the way places such as under your bed or the piano. In fact, people have all sorts of weird names for these globs of dust: fuzzballs, dust puppies.

Did you notice any difference in the size of the dust particles on the floor compared to those high up on a bookshelf?

Dust is so light that the slightest movement of air pushes it around. It collects only where there are few or no air currents. What does the distribution of dust puppies tell you about the microwinds in your house? Where is the least visited, least known spot in the house according to the dusty evidence?

How long does it take for dust to collect in a spot? Devise a test to see.

What effect does static electricity have on dust?

Make a list of the different kinds of stuff in your dust.

4

House
Happenings

Part 4
House Happenings

Magic Doorway

The threshold or doorway has special meaning in many places. It marks the change from the indoors to the world outside. And in our climate-controlled world this shift from the outdoors to indoor spring can be magical.

In the old days, passing through the doorway was sort of like rebirth. If you have ever stumbled out the door half asleep in the early morning on your way to school, you know going out can be a little like being born all over again.

Stumbling over the threshold is bad luck in many places. Stepping on or kicking the threshold is also bad luck. The right way to cross is to step over the threshold with the right foot in front of the left. The right side of the body is considered stronger than the left in the places where this custom is important.

Of course, we have forgotten about all this silly magic stuff, almost. We still say it's important to get off on the right foot. And brides are still being carried over the threshold, even though few could tell you

why. Sometimes animals were placed at either side of the door to guard it. Even today you sometimes see a pair of magnificent beasts lounging on either side of the doors of a bank, a public building, or a fancy house. Nowadays these animal statues are backed up by heavy-duty locks.

Sign of the Shoe

Sometimes you will run across a horseshoe nailed to a house or a barn. Horseshoes are supposed to be lucky. This is a very old tradition. There are a lot of stories about why it got started. One is that the early Christians marked their doors with a special symbol so they would know each other in the ancient days when it was dangerous to be Christian. A horseshoe tipped to the side was the first letter of the name Christ.

There is also a legend about St. Dustan who tangled with the devil. He overpowered the demon then nailed his hoof to a barn. Another theory is that the horseshoe is a symbol of the headdress of Isis. This ancient Egyptian goddess of fertility was considered a mother and protector. Her symbol kept a house safe. Like many traditions with magical roots, the exact origins are lost. However, it's safe to say people like decorations and have a lust for good luck.

P.S. If you hang a horseshoe, hang it with the ends up so the luck can't run out.

Divine Fire

Early people somehow knew that light from the sun was a life-giving power. Darkness, the opposite of light, was a thing to be feared. Light came to be a symbol for the forces of good; darkness symbolized the forces of fear and evil.

Fire, too, became a symbol of life and the life-giving properties of light. It has played an important part in the religions of many people. In ancient Rome priestesses called vestal virgins devoted their lives to tending the sacred fire, which honored Vesta, goddess of the hearth. At the end of the year the fire was extinguished, then in a ritual at the beginning of the new year her special fire was rekindled.

The Egyptians and Syrians also kept a sacred fire in every village. Even today in some churches and temples special flames are kept burning throughout the year.

The Yule log, or Christmas fire, comes from the ancient Teutonic midwinter feast. The lighting of fire was a magical ceremony that was done to give strength to the weak winter sun. In December Jews celebrate Hanukkah, an eight-day festival of lights; and many people decorate their homes with candles and lights at Christmastime.

Fire Signs

Fire still has a magical quality. It is easy to sit back and see pictures in the flames and let them suggest stories. Fires have been thought to foretell the future. In some places they are read like tea leaves. Read on for some omens that have been used to decode what is written in the flames.

If you find that these omens just aren't describing your fire very well, there may be an excellent reason. The meanings for most of these omens originally came from England, a country where the fires are generally made with coal. Perhaps you will have to make up some new omen descriptions and meanings that will work well with a wood fire or with charcoal briquets.

A FIRE ON ONE SIDE OR ONE THAT FALLS INTO TWO PARTS MEANS A PARTING.

A FIRE THAT WON'T START SIGNALS A QUARREL TO COME.

A FLYING, COFFIN-SHAPED CINDER FORE-TELLS A DEATH. A CRADLE SHAPE FORE-TELLS A BIRTH.

A CLUSTER OF BRIGHT SPARKS MEANS GOOD NEWS. DULL SPARKS ARE BAD NEWS.

IF A COAL FALLS AT SOMEONE'S FEET, IT MEANS A WEDDING IS IN STORE.

A COAL EXPLODING IN YOUR DIRECTION MEANS THAT YOU HAVE AN ENEMY.

IF THE FIRE BLAZES UP, A STRANGER IS NEAR.

A BUZZING FIRE MEANS A TEMPEST IS NEAR. LEAPING ASHES MEAN RAIN.

Fireplace Suction

A fireplace sucks a lot of air from the room inside your house and sends it up the chimney. You can test this yourself the next time there is a fire in your fireplace or a friend's fireplace.

You will need a long match or a slender piece of wood. Light the tip. Now blow it out so that you get a stream of smoke from the end. This is your tracking device for the air that streams up the chimney.

How far can you hold the match from the fireplace and still see that the smoke is being pulled into the chimney? How fast does it go? Does it make any difference if the fire is burning brightly or if it is only hot coals? What happens when there is no fire?

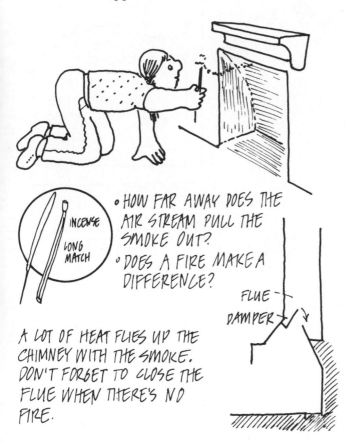

INCENSE
LONG MATCH

○ HOW FAR AWAY DOES THE AIR STREAM PULL THE SMOKE OUT?
○ DOES A FIRE MAKE A DIFFERENCE?

FLUE
DAMPER

A LOT OF HEAT FLIES UP THE CHIMNEY WITH THE SMOKE. DON'T FORGET TO CLOSE THE FLUE WHEN THERE'S NO FIRE.

Fireplace Food

If you are lucky enough to have a fireplace at your house, you could think about using it as a place to cook dinner. It is a fun thing to do, especially if you are in the mood for a picnic and the weather won't let you go outside. Cooking on the hearth is an ancient and honorable way to prepare food. In the old days all food was cooked that way.

There are two basic ways to cook food in the fireplace. One is to singe the food in flames. High flames make a cool fire. The other way is to wait for the fire to burn down to coals. These coals are a hotter fire with more even heat.

Hot Fruit

1. Cut up fresh fruit into chunks. You can use apples, pears, berries, peaches, plums. Whatever you like. Cut denser fruit such as apples in smaller chunks.

2. Place the fruit chunks on a double layer of aluminum foil.

3. Sprinkle with cinnamon. Drip some honey on top if you like your fruit sweet.

FRUIT

FOIL

CAREFUL OPENING, THE FOIL WHEN IT'S DONE!

ROLL IT UP.

ROLL THE OTHER ENDS.

4. Wrap two sides together, then the other two sides. Make it tight so no juice can get out.

5. Place the fruit seam-side up on the hot coals for about 15 minutes.

6. Remove the fruit from the fire and carefully unwrap. Eat it plain or pour it over ice cream or cake. It is wonderful.

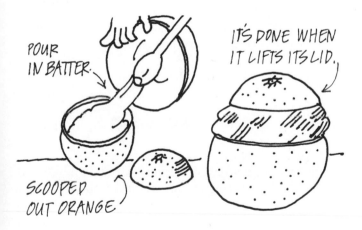

POUR IN BATTER.

IT'S DONE WHEN IT LIFTS ITS LID.

SCOOPED OUT ORANGE

Orange Cupcake

1. Cut the top off a big orange with a thick skin. Save the top.

2. Scoop out the orange meat with a spoon.

3. Make some yellow, white, or chocolate batter. Pour enough into the hollow orange to fill it one-third full. Put on the top.

4. Set the orange in the hot coals.

5. It is done when the lid is lifted by the cake.

6. Pull it out of the fire and dig into orange-flavored cake. Careful, it's hot.

BATTER

FRUIT CHUNKS AT THE BOTTOM

TIE ON FOIL.

COOK ON A GRATE.

SLIDE IT OUT WHEN IT'S DONE. CAREFUL, IT'S HOT!

Can Cake

1. Put some pineapple chunks, fruit cocktail, or other drained, canned fruit in the bottom of a coffee can.

2. Make some yellow cake batter. Fill the can about one-half full of batter.

3. Put on a foil top. Make it tight.

4. Set the can on a grate in the fire. Arrange the coals around the can. Let it cook for about 45 minutes.

5. Take the can out of the fire with tongs. Turn it upside down and dig in.

TORTILLA
PEANUT BUTTER

ROLL UP THE TORTILLA.

WRAP IT UP AND COOK IT ON COALS.

Weird and Wonderful Peanut Butter and Jelly Burritos

1. Spread a flour tortilla with peanut butter and jelly. Put on a bit more jelly than peanut butter to keep it moist.
2. Roll it up.
3. Wrap it in aluminum foil.
4. Put it on hot coals for about 10 minutes.
5. Be careful unwrapping this hot number.

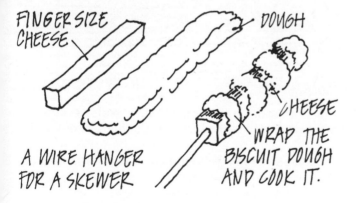

FINGER SIZE CHEESE

DOUGH

CHEESE

A WIRE HANGER FOR A SKEWER

WRAP THE BISCUIT DOUGH AND COOK IT.

Wraparound Doughboys

1. Cut cheddar cheese into finger-size pieces.
2. Stick them on metal skewers. Wire clothes hangers that have been opened up will work fine.

3. Wrap the cheese fingers with biscuit dough. Or you can use canned crescent rolls.
4. Roast the doughboy over hot coals until it is crusty on the outside.

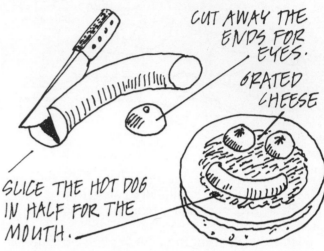

CUT AWAY THE ENDS FOR EYES.

GRATED CHEESE

SLICE THE HOT DOG IN HALF FOR THE MOUTH.

Open-Faced Fools

1. Split an English muffin.
2. Sprinkle with grated cheese.
3. Make eyes and a mouth out of slices of a hot dog.
4. Toast the fool over the coals.

All Burned Up

Have you ever sat next to a roaring fire and wondered what was going on inside to turn a chunk of wood into a flashy light show with sound effects?

Burning is nothing more than oxygen atoms combining with the atoms in a chunk of wood. A fire is oxidation in a hurry. This oxidation happens so fast that noticeable heat and light are produced. We see flames, the glowing fire, and feel heat.

What is the difference between the logs setting in the woodbox and the ones flaming in the fireplace?

Why don't all pieces of wood burst into flames and start oxidizing in the air of their own accord?

Atoms have to get excited before they will burn. This excitement is started by applying a little heat to the substance that you wish to burn. The atoms on the surface of a log start to vibrate when they are heated up. They vibrate faster and faster until they start to break apart. The atoms of oxygen, carbon, and hydrogen in the wood begin flying apart in all directions. As this happens, oxygen in the air starts combining with these loose molecules. Heat and light and sounds are produced. The wood is on fire.

As the piece of wood burns, a lot of new substances are formed. You get water, carbon dioxide, methane, pentane, hexane, and octane—plus heat, light, and sound. A piece of burning wood is like a chemical factory.

Oxidation

Oxygen is an active element. It likes to combine with other substances and is constantly doing so. This joining process is called oxidation. Oxidation is going on all around you.

Rust, for instance, is made by oxidation: iron joining up with oxygen. The surfaces of iron objects are constantly hooking up with oxygen. The results are reddish brown flakes that are the curse of the mechanical world. People give iron surfaces a protective skin of paint to foil these attractive oxygen molecules. The drying of paint is also oxidation—a case of fighting oxidation with oxidation.

A slice of apple turning brown in the air is oxidation. A copper pot turning dark is oxidation. A newspaper doesn't turn yellow and brittle with age. A newspaper turns yellow and brittle with oxygen. That's right. The molecules are combining with oxygen. It's kind of a slow burn.

Soot

After the fire is over you will notice that there are a few things left behind. One of these things is a gray powder called ash. Ash is made up mostly of minerals that don't burn. In fact, gardeners sometimes put ash on their gardens as a source of minerals for their plants.

Another item left behind after the fire is the black sooty stuff that sticks to the walls of the chimney. This soot is carbon that hasn't been oxidized. It can build up in a fireplace and choke the inside of the chimney.

In the old days when fire was an everyday occurrence, this sooty coating needed to be cleaned every so often. It was a hard job since a chimney is like a long, skinny up-and-down tunnel. Sometimes a goose was stuffed up the chimney. The mad flapping of wings cleaned the inside. When no geese were about, kids were sometimes used. In exchange for a few pennies a child would crawl up the inside of the chimney with a broom and sweep out the soot. These small workers were called chimney sweeps. Chimney cleaning was hard on both kids and geese.

Secret Message

If you are burning with the desire to send a secret message, here is a way to do it. All you need is a little juice or milk, a secret message-writing instrument, and a sheet of paper. Reading the message takes a little magic performed by a light bulb, which is also known as a chemical reaction.

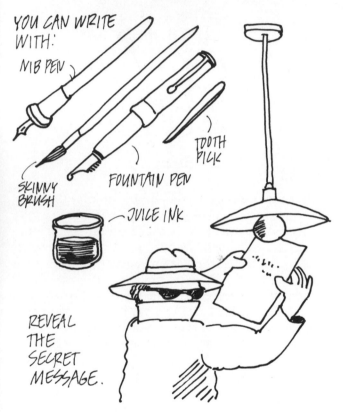

YOU CAN WRITE WITH:

NIB PEN

SKINNY BRUSH

FOUNTAIN PEN

TOOTH PICK

JUICE INK

REVEAL THE SECRET MESSAGE.

1. Pour a little lemon or orange juice in a small jar. This is the ink.

2. Find a skinny brush or an old-fashioned pen for a writing tool. In a pinch you could use a toothpick.

3. Write the message on the paper. Let it dry.

4. To read the message hold the paper next to a light bulb. The invisible ink will carbonize on the paper and reveal your words.

Afraid of the Dark?

How many times have you laughed at someone little because he or she was afraid to go into a dark spot? Why do little kids like to go to sleep with the light on? Have you noticed that lots of chiller, thriller tales start with the line, "It was a dark and moonless night"?

If you stay out late, someone will probably leave the porch light on until you are safely home.

Why will most people put up with an annoying streetlight shining in their window at night? They would rather have the light. It makes them feel safe. The truth is that a lot of us are a little bit afraid of the dark.

CHIMNEY SWIFTS MAKE A GLUE WITH WHICH THEY STICK THEIR NESTS TO WALLS. THEY USED TO NEST IN HOLLOW TREES; NOW THEY ARE MORE COMMON IN CHIMNEYS. THEIR ASIAN COUSINS MAKE THE NESTS THAT THE CHINESE COOK INTO SOUP.

Candle Chemistry

Did you know that the smoke of candles will burn? You can prove it for yourself.

1. Light the candle.
2. Puff out the flame.
3. Quickly put a lighted match into the smoky streak.
4. A flame will shoot down.

In fact, you are not really burning a candle, you are burning carbon gas. This is how it happens. When a candle is lighted, the heat from the match melts some of the wax. Because wax is a liquid, it travels up the wick. The heat of the candle flame turns the liquid wax into a gas. It is when this gas burns that you see the yellow flame.

If you blow out the flame, you get a stream of smoky stuff. The stream of smoke is actually tiny drops of wax that were just a moment ago a gas. That's why the smoke turns to flame again.

You can stick a strip of metal into the tip of the flame of a candle to catch some black carbon atoms before they have a chance to burn up. Hold a strip of aluminum foil in the tip of a candle flame. The black smudge on the foil is made of carbon atoms.

Candle wax is a carbon compound. As the candle becomes a gas, carbon atoms are released. They are oxidized to carbon dioxide by the flame and glow with heat and light. The foil lets you catch some carbon atoms before they are oxidized. WARNING: ASK AN ADULT TO HELP YOU WITH THIS EXPERIMENT.

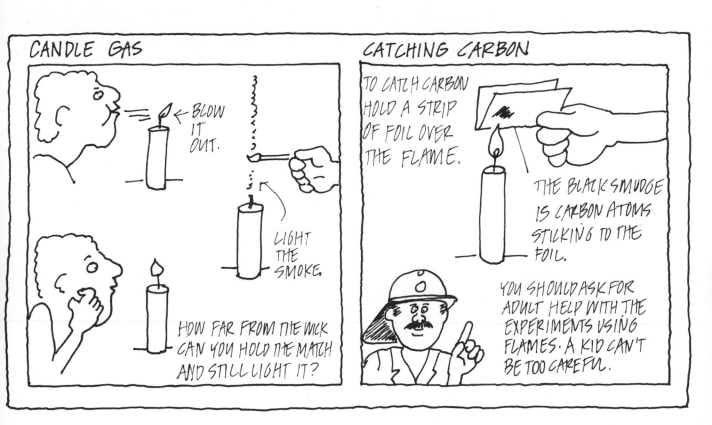

CANDLE GAS

BLOW IT OUT.

LIGHT THE SMOKE.

HOW FAR FROM THE WICK CAN YOU HOLD THE MATCH AND STILL LIGHT IT?

CATCHING CARBON

TO CATCH CARBON HOLD A STRIP OF FOIL OVER THE FLAME.

THE BLACK SMUDGE IS CARBON ATOMS STICKING TO THE FOIL.

YOU SHOULD ASK FOR ADULT HELP WITH THE EXPERIMENTS USING FLAMES. A KID CAN'T BE TOO CAREFUL.

Picture a Flame

There are three basic zones of activity inside a flame. You can see them if you look closely. Test them with a trial by fire.

1. Cut a piece of white cardboard.
2. Carefully put it into the flame for three or four seconds. Hold it still.
3. Remove it quickly before it catches fire.
4. You may have to repeat this a couple of times to make a good flame print.

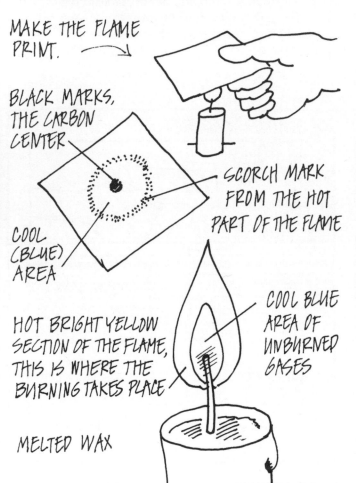

MAKE THE FLAME PRINT.

BLACK MARKS, THE CARBON CENTER

COOL (BLUE) AREA

SCORCH MARK FROM THE HOT PART OF THE FLAME

HOT BRIGHT YELLOW SECTION OF THE FLAME, THIS IS WHERE THE BURNING TAKES PLACE

COOL BLUE AREA OF UNBURNED GASES

MELTED WAX

Energy

Not too long ago energy was something that you either had or didn't have. If you were too tired to keep your eyes open, you were out of energy. If you woke up ready to climb a mountain, you were bursting with it.

Today when people say energy, they usually mean gasoline or electricity or whether something is energy efficient. There is also a lot of talk about solar energy, wind energy, energy waste, energy this and energy that.

What is all this talk about energy? What is energy anyway?

Energy is the ability to do work. It comes in many forms: water running downhill, fuels to be burned, electricity flowing through wires. Energy is nothing new. It's been around forever. People have known about it for a long time.

For a while it looked as if there were as much energy as we could ever want just waiting to be plugged into. We started using it for powering electric toothbrushes, little machines to grind coffee beans, a car for everybody in the family, electric music machines, electric socks, sitdown lawn mowers, machines to make bubbles in the bathtub. Inventive minds figured out a way to use energy for just about everything. However, that was before we noticed that, like almost everything else, energy comes in a nonreturnable, limited supply.

These days people are reminded by their pocketbooks that energy isn't free. We knew it all along, it's just that we forgot for a while.

Saving Energy

Most of the energy in your house gets used up by the climate-making machines in it. A whopping 70 percent of the energy used at home goes for heating and cooling your space. The next biggest chunk is the energy that goes for heating your shower, bath, and wash water. That amounts to another 20 percent. That leaves 10 percent for the lights, the TV, and the other small machines.

You can see that turning off the lights and switching off the TV set isn't going to make a big dent in your energy use. The key to saving energy around the house is at the thermostat. If you keep the thermostat on the heater at 68 degrees in the winter and the air conditioner at 72 to 78 degrees in the summer, you can save from 12 to 47 percent of your energy costs. Here are some tried and true ways to make up the difference. They are a bit old-fashioned, but they work.

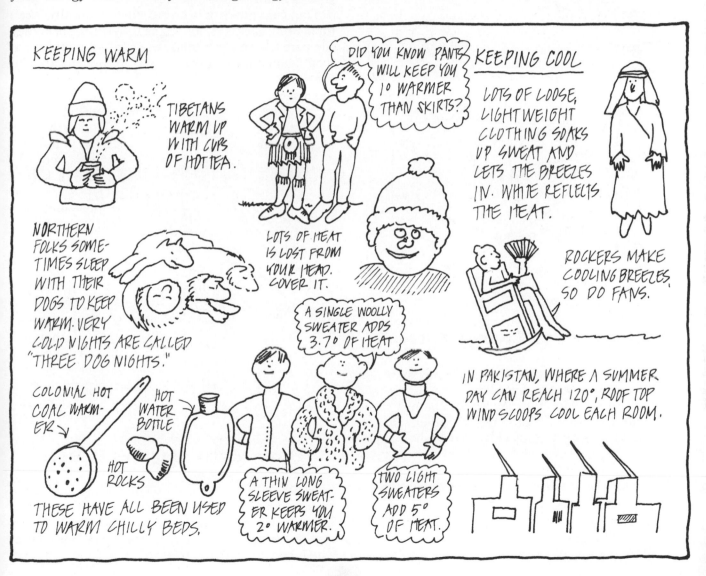

Send Away: Energy Poster

If you would like to think about energy, you can get a big, colorful poster to hang on your wall. On one side is a game called "Pull the Plug." You play using the poster as a game board. On the other side is a poster called "Solar Energy: Day and Night." It pictures some spacy, solar inventions and gives instructions for a solar hot dog cooker.

Write for the activity poster number 245, "Solar Energy." Send $2.30 to:

Springhouse Corporation
1111 Bethlehem Pike
Springhouse, Pennsylvania 19477

A Blanket Is Not Hot

"Put on your nice warm jacket so you won't get cold when you go outside."

It's not your jacket that is warm. *You* are the hot stuff. The jacket is just a kind of envelope that holds your heat inside your clothes.

You can prove it to yourself and anyone who thinks your jacket is hot. Take its temperature, then compare it with other things at your house that are at room temperature. Like the pots in the kitchen. Or the down sleeping bag. Or the living room sofa. Or the inside of the bathtub.

You might be surprised at what you find.

How Many Degrees Is Hot?

So how is it that your fat woolly coat is about the same number of degrees as the inside of the bathtub? If you had a choice of sitting naked in your woolly coat or the bathtub on a cool day, there is no doubt which one you would choose.

Why are you sure to freeze your fanny in the bathtub and to stay toasty warm in your woolly coat if they are both the same temperature?

The difference is in the heat-holding ability of these two materials. The woolly sweater soaks up heat and holds it. The bathtub lets heat go very quickly. Things such as bathtubs and metal surfaces are said to be good conductors of heat. They conduct it away from your surface very fast. Then you feel cold. The sweater, on the other hand, is a poor conductor. It holds your body heat to you, and you feel toasty warm.

What do degrees measure? They are a measure of the amount of heat. Or, more precisely, how fast are the atoms moving inside the thing? That is different altogether from how well or how long a thing can hold heat.

Send Away:
Natural Gas Facts

Did you know that in ancient times some early people found a burning spring of natural gas and worshipped its flames? Today in the United States there are more than one million miles of natural gas pipeline. Did you know that these big lines cost almost one million dollars per mile? Natural gas is pretty important stuff. Find out all this and more in "Gilmore's Guide to Natural Gas." This colorful booklet is available for students who write:

Educational Programs
American Gas Association
1515 Wilson Boulevard
Arlington, Virginia 22209

HIDE THE COIN BET-
WEEN YOUR FINGERS.

ARRANGE THE HANKIE.

PULL THE HANKIE TIGHT

PRESS THE HOT STICK AGAINST THE COIN.

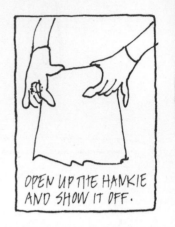

OPEN UP THE HANKIE AND SHOW IT OFF.

Conduct Some Magic

You press the red-hot stick against the lily-white hankie. You open the hankie and show it to the audience. There is not even the slightest burn. How do you perform this magic?

You have hidden a quarter behind the hankie. You know that heat from the poker will travel to the coin so fast that the hankie is spared from burning. You know that metal is a very good conductor of heat. But, of course, your audience doesn't know that. They think it's magic — and in a way it is.

Here is how to present this illusion:

1. Set up a table with your magic stuff. You need a dowel, a hankie, and a candle in a holder.

2. Show the audience each piece of your equipment. Explain that they are all perfectly ordinary things. Pass them around if they don't believe you.

3. Light the candle. Heat the tip of the dowel until it is very hot. Explain to the audience that the dowel is getting hotter and hotter and how you are going to plunge it into the heart of a white hankie. Tell them how under less magical circumstances you might expect a big brown hole in the hankie.

4. Pick up the hankie. Show the audience both sides. Don't show them the quarter you have hidden in one hand.

5. This is the tricky part. Wad up the hankie in one hand, slipping the quarter inside.

6. With lots of fanfare press the hot dowel into the hankie. Make sure it is pressing against the quarter.

7. Open the cloth, concealing the quarter. Let the audience have a closer look.

8. Take a bow.

Send Away:
Celsius Hot, Celsius Cold

It's a real scorcher today. It's 38 degrees in the shade — sounds cuckoo until you realize it means 38 degrees Celsius. The easiest way to learn Celsius degrees is to stop trying to think of the Fahrenheit degrees. If you know that 38 degrees in the shade is hotter than Hades, you can stop trying to convert to Fahrenheit degrees.

There is a colorful poster called "Celsius Hot, Celsius Cold" that has all kinds of useful information on the Celsius scale. The flip side has another poster called "A New Way to Weigh" and it is chock-full of interesting metric information and facts. You might also ask for a list of the other nifty learning posters that this company makes. Ask for Activity Poster number 244. It costs $2.30 from:

Springhouse Corporation
1111 Bethlehem Pike
Springhouse, Pennsylvania 19477

Send Away: Aunt Energina

If you want to sharpen your energy sense, read "The Adventures of Aunt Energina." This mild-mannered granny, along with Clarence, her bionic cat, turns into a ferocious fighter of waste once she puts on her lightning bolt apron. This comic book has adventures and puzzles, plus instructions on how to make a water turbine and an electromagnet, how to hold a home energy investigation, and more.

You might be able to get a free copy from your local power company. Prices for classroom sets are available from:

Innovative Communications
P.O. Box 23205
Pleasant Hill, California 94523

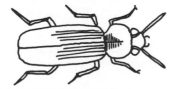

DOES YOUR FURNITURE TICK? IT IS POSSIBLE THAT IT IS HOME FOR THE WOOD-BORING FURNITURE BEETLE. LOOK FOR SMALL HOLES AND SAWDUST AND AVOID SITTING ON A TICKING CHAIR.

Creaks Speak

Shhh! What was that? Did you hear that noise?

A lot of times late at night you hear creaks and thumps and groanings and squeakings. They can be sort of scary, especially if you are home alone. Where are those weird noises coming from? Is your house haunted? Should you call the police?

Squeaks and creaks are not generally a matter for the police. They are most likely the sounds of your house settling down for the night. During the day the house heats up. The materials in the house expand when they are heated. After dark the house cools off, and the materials in the house shrink. The results of this expanding and shrinking are heard as pops and creaks and squeaks. The reason you hear them only late at night is that in most houses the noises from the activity of the day drown them out. Also, maybe late at night you are listening a little harder for strange noises. If you listen, you may notice that your house makes noises all day long. Some houses make such regular noises that you can tell the time of day by the sounds of expansion and shrinking—the creaks act like a clock.

Pay attention, your house may be speaking to you.

Ordinary Extraordinary Fluid

Water is the most ordinary fluid. You cook your food in it. You lap up glasses of it every day. You use it to turn lemonade powder into a drink. It cleans the dirt off your shirts. You shower yourself with it. People at the beach sit by it, swim in it, and sail on it. They fill squirt guns with it. People have fought wars over it.

The only thing you don't do is think about it. How much do you know about this stuff you use a hundred different ways?

Clouds in the Kitchen

Right there over the pot of hot soup or above the hot shower you are likely to see some clouds: indoor weather in the making. It's possible you have seen these indoor clouds and dismissed them as steam, never thinking that they are the very same creations as the clouds that float over the landscape outside your windows.

Both are related to the amount of water vapor in the air and they're both made the same way. When the molecules of water are subjected to enough heat, they get excited. They start leaping around. Some of them break away from the liquid and fly off into the air. This process is called evaporation. A cloud is a collection of water droplets in the air — water vapor condensed into drops.

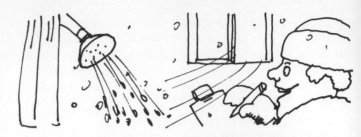

Snow in the Shower

Reading books you might get the idea that science is a long series of successes. Not true.

Science is mostly failures, sprinkled with an occasional success. Usually you don't hear about the failures.

Here is a spectacular failure story told by a scientist who conducted the following experiment in college. He tried to make it snow indoors.

"On the coldest night of the winter, when it was about 20 degrees below zero Fahrenheit outside, I closed the door to our dormitory bathroom and opened all the bathroom windows. It was Saturday night, and I remember the dorm was deserted except for me. After some time, roughly an hour, the temperature in the bathroom had fallen to about 5 degrees below zero Fahrenheit. Then I turned on all the hot water faucets in the showers, thinking that the fine spray would crystallize and turn to snow as the steam rose. Instead, it condensed on the walls and stalls of the bathroom. In fact, after about 15 minutes, the entire bathroom was coated with a layer of ice. You can imagine the surprise of my roommates when they returned from their dates and found a frozen bathroom. The identity of the culprit was quickly discovered, and I was taken to the graduate resident in charge of our floor, who had virtually no sense of humor. This experiment was performed before the era of modern snowmaking equipment."

Nowadays this scientist does mostly theoretical science. That's the kind that is mathematics, written on paper or blackboards.

Hot, Humid Stickies

Have you ever noticed that some days your drawers stick and other days they open and close with no resistance? When they stick, your drawers have sucked up water from the air. Wood is a material that will actually change size according to how much water it is holding. On a humid day your drawer will drink up water vapor from the air. It becomes fat and swollen. In dry weather the water gets sucked out of (evaporates from) the wood, and the drawer shrinks.

Water Quiz

1. How does it freeze? From the outside in or from the inside out?
2. How does it get to the tops of trees?
3. Does it take up more space or less when it turns into ice?
4. What color is it?
5. When frozen does it sink or float?
6. Why does it boil at exactly 100 degrees and freeze at 0 degrees on the centigrade thermometer?

See page 100 for the answers.

Indoor Desert

Drawers are not the only things that get the water sucked out of them in dry weather. Water gets sucked out of your body too. Remember those dry, chapped lips and the uncomfortable sting of air in your nose in really dry weather? The moisture is moving from your body into the surrounding air. This can happen on a hot, dry, dusty day in the summer, or anytime you happen to be in the Sahara Desert. It can also happen to you right inside your room in the wintertime.

The science of how a perfectly ordinary house in December can end up as dry as the Sahara goes like this. Air is able to hold different amounts of water at different temperatures. The higher the temperature, the more water vapor it can hold. For instance, 72-degree air can hold 11 times more water than air at 10 degrees. Most heaters today take air from the outside, heat it, and send it around inside the house. In the winter they take cold air that contains only a little water, heat it, and send it into your room. As your house gets very warm, this same air begins to feel like a desert wind. And it acts like the desert wind, sucking the moisture out of everything it touches. Wood shrinks, the plaster cracks, lips crack, and the piano goes out of tune. Not only that, the water that is being removed from your surface by this very dry air is making you cool. A person can lower the heat in a humid room and feel warmer. On the other hand, a person in a dry room needs to turn up the heat in order to stay warm—getting even drier in the process. It's what you call a vicious circle.

DURING THE HEATING SEASON THE AVERAGE AMERICAN HOME CAN HAVE A RELATIVE HUMIDITY OF 13%. THAT'S ABOUT TWICE AS DRY AS THE SAHARA DESERT.

Answers to Water Quiz

1. From the outside in. Anybody who has ever poked a finger in the ice cube tray to see if the ice is ready yet, when it isn't quite frozen, knows that. However, you might not know that this peculiar property of freezing from the outside in keeps our world from freezing over. Ice is an excellent insulator. When it covers the seas and land, it actually forms a blanket that holds heat in. Otherwise, the seas would freeze solid.

2. No one has ever quite figured out that one. You would be partly right if you said capillary action.

3. It takes up more space, it expands.

4. You could say colorless, but a real expert knows that it has a slightly bluish tinge.

5. Float. That one was easy, but can you explain why?

6. Because the centigrade scale is based on the freezing and boiling points of water.

How did you do? How much do you know about water? Water might be an ordinary liquid, but it often acts in extraordinary ways — ways that are very important to life on this planet. Coming up is a series of experiments you can do to find out firsthand about this ordinary extraordinary stuff.

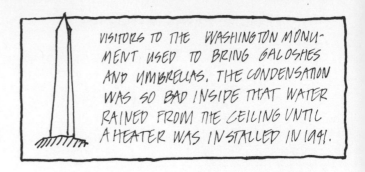

VISITORS TO THE WASHINGTON MONUMENT USED TO BRING GALOSHES AND UMBRELLAS. THE CONDENSATION WAS SO BAD INSIDE THAT WATER RAINED FROM THE CEILING UNTIL A HEATER WAS INSTALLED IN 1941.

Rain on the Windows

To stay alive a cloud needs heat. Those water vapor molecules need to continue bouncing around in an excited motion in order to remain in a gaseous state. When the temperature drops, much of the water gives up being a gas really fast. It literally falls right out of the sky — as rain. In the case of an indoor cloud, if it runs into a cold, solid surface, it will transform itself into a liquid right on the spot. That's when you get rain on the windows. Another name for this quick-change process is condensation.

Hair Hygrometer

If you know somebody who has long hair, you can make a machine to measure how much water is in the air. Magic? No. It's a simple device that puts the shrinking and swelling effects to work. Hair shrinks or lengthens depending on the amount of moisture in the air. You can read the results. Now you know why some people have curly hair on rainy days.

You need a human hair at least 10 inches long, a milk carton, a broom straw, a paper clip, a needle, a penny, some tape, glue, and a sheet of paper.

1. Wash the milk carton with soap and water. Wipe the hair with rubbing alcohol. Let them dry.

2. Cut an "H" in the side of the carton. A single edge razor blade or a mat knife are good tools for this job. Fold up the flaps.

3. Insert the needle into the flaps. Twist it around so that it moves freely.

4. Punch a paper clip at the top of the carton so it lines up with the needle.

5. Tape the penny to the end of the hair. Try to handle the hair as little as possible so no oil from your fingers rubs off on it.

6. Wrap the hair around the needle once and attach it to the paper clip with a drop of glue.

7. Make the chart. Tape it to the side under the needle.

8. Thread the broom straw through the eye of the needle to make the pointer.

9. You need to set your hygrometer for 100 percent humidity. Take it to the bathroom and turn on the shower to get the room steamy. When the pointer stops moving, gently push it to the number 10.

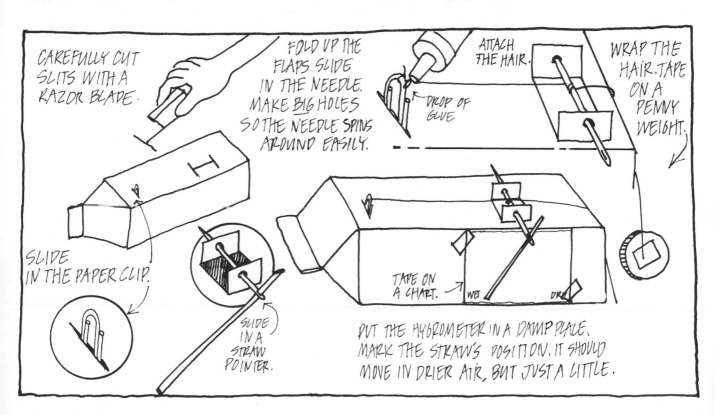

CAREFULLY CUT SLITS WITH A RAZOR BLADE.

FOLD UP THE FLAPS. SLIDE IN THE NEEDLE. MAKE <u>BIG</u> HOLES SO THE NEEDLE SPINS AROUND EASILY.

ATTACH THE HAIR.

DROP OF GLUE

WRAP THE HAIR. TAPE ON A PENNY WEIGHT.

SLIDE IN THE PAPER CLIP.

SLIDE IN A STRAW POINTER.

TAPE ON A CHART.

WET   DRY

PUT THE HYGROMETER IN A DAMP PLACE. MARK THE STRAW'S POSITION. IT SHOULD MOVE IN DRIER AIR, BUT JUST A LITTLE.

The Three States That Matter

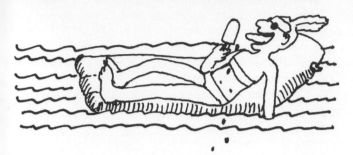

You might already know this stuff. If so, just skip ahead. If you don't, hang onto your hat because we're getting ready to discuss a bit of atomic theory.

Why do kids need to bother with atomic theory? Well, they don't, but if you want to know about the nature of things, knowing a bit about how atoms behave will help explain a lot of mysteries.

Take water, for instance. You know it can be an invisible part of air. Or a fat, fluffy, free-floating cloud. Or a rock-hard chunk of ice. Or a quicksilver liquid. How can the same substance act so many different ways? The answer is in the molecules or, more precisely, in the motions of the molecules that make up water.

These tiny particles respond to temperature and pressure. The more heat and pressure, the faster they move and the more unstable they are. These wild, fast-moving molecules are a gas. When they are slowed down by a big drop in temperature or pressure, or both, these same molecules become a solid mass: ice. The same molecules at different rates of motion make up the different states of matter.

Water Crawls

That's right. Water just naturally crawls up tubes. It can lift itself up great distances against the force of gravity. This peculiar behavior is called capillary action.

1. FILL A GLASS HALF FULL OF WATER. ADD A BIT OF RED COLOR.

2. SLICE THE ROOT END OFF A CELERY STALK. PUT IT IN THE WATER.

3. COME BACK LATER AND LOOK FOR EVIDENCE OF CAPILLARY ACTION.

Pour yourself a glass of water. If you look very closely, you will notice that the water curves up against the side of the glass. It is this little lifting action that lets water crawl up thin tubes.

The oxygen molecules in water are attracted to the oxygen molecules in the glass. Thin tubes have more surface to attract the water. While the water is being lifted along the surface of the tube, surface tension tries to keep the surface of the water smooth like a tight skin. These opposing forces cause the water to crawl up the walls.

It's a lucky thing, too, for it is this action that accounts at least partially for the movement of water through soils and plants.

Two-Tone Flowers

You can make some wild and wonderful two-tone flowers with the help of capillary action.

1. Set up two glasses of water. Put different colors in each of them.

2. Find some white flowers. Carnations are good.

3. With a knife or scissors carefully split the stems lengthwise.

4. Put one half of each stem into one glass and the other half into the second glass. Wait for the two-tone flowers.

SPLIT THE STEM IN HALF.

DIFFERENT COLORED WATER

Teakettle Rain

This teakettle process of distillation is a miniature version of the rain cycle. When heat is applied to the water, it turns itself into a cloud. When it lands in a cool environment, the cloud condenses into water drops or raindrops.

In the following experiment the aluminum foil sheet acts as a cool surface because of its high thermal conductivity.

1. Put some water in a teakettle.

2. Put the kettle on the stove and bring the water to a boil.

3. Hold a sheet of aluminum foil above the spout of the teakettle to catch some of the steam. The foil should be large enough so you can keep your fingers out of the way of the steam.

4. The steam will condense on the foil and drip off the edge. Catch this "rain" in a cup.

When the water evaporates, it leaves behind the impurities to set in the bottom of the kettle, so the remaining result is pure water. This separating process is called distillation. People have been thinking for a long time about distilling sea water where fresh water is scarce. The problem is that the heat energy it would take to distill sea water would make the end product pretty expensive. Perhaps you can think of a way to distill sea water and revolutionize the water business.

USE A MITT AND BE CAREFUL OF YOUR FINGERS.

TRY A WATER TASTE TEST.

The Force of Expanding Water

Most liquids shrink when they freeze. Water does just the opposite. The reason water expands when it freezes is locked in its crystal structure. The frozen molecules of water fit together into a crystal structure that is like a long pyramid. In this position they make a light, airy structure that has a microspace locked inside. It is this trapped space that makes ice such a good insulator, and makes it take up more room than in the liquid form.

Crystals to Eat

PAPER CUP

WOODEN OR PLASTIC SPOON

ICE CUBE TRAY POPS WITH PLASTIC STRAW HANDLES

CAN YOU EAT FAST ENOUGH TO BEAT THE PHASE CHANGE?

CUT THE STRAWS IN HALF FOR HANDLES.

You have a machine in your house that is built to slow down the movement of atomic particles. It is called a refrigerator. In the interior of its freezer compartment you can turn watery liquids to solids. Put some atomic theory to use; you can eat the results.

1. Pick out a can of your favorite frozen fruit juice.
2. Mix the juice with water. Put in a little less water than it calls for on the directions so your frozen suckers will have a snappier flavor.

3. Pour the juice into small paper cups.
4. Set the cups in the freezer.
5. When crystals start to form, stick in some wooden sticks or plastic spoons for handles.
6. When the juice has turned to solid crystals, they are ready to eat. Peel off the paper and take a bite.

Can you eat the frozen sucker fast enough to beat the phase change from solid crystals to liquid?

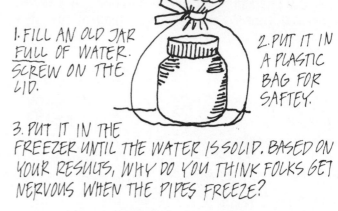

1. FILL AN OLD JAR FULL OF WATER. SCREW ON THE LID.

2. PUT IT IN A PLASTIC BAG FOR SAFTEY.

3. PUT IT IN THE FREEZER UNTIL THE WATER IS SOLID. BASED ON YOUR RESULTS, WHY DO YOU THINK FOLKS GET NERVOUS WHEN THE PIPES FREEZE?

Anatomy of a Plumbing System

Plumbing is not generally considered one of your more fascinating subjects. Most people don't know anything about their personal set of pipes that send a supply of sparkling clean, clear water gushing out of their faucets. Contrary to popular opinion, plumbing can be interesting. For instance, did you know that your pipes are equipped with a set of traps to prevent the dreaded sewer gas from creeping into your house? Did you know that a plumbing system is actually four different systems? One brings water into the house, one is for hot water, one sends waste water into the sewer, and one brings air into the system so the other systems will flow. Have a look at the chart and learn a bit about your pipes.

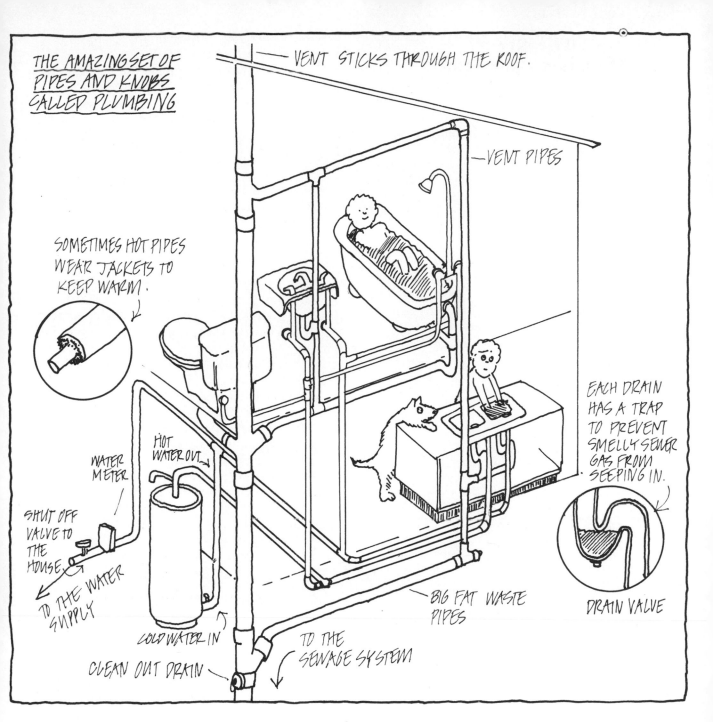

THE AMAZING SET OF PIPES AND KNOBS CALLED PLUMBING

VENT STICKS THROUGH THE ROOF.

VENT PIPES

SOMETIMES HOT PIPES WEAR JACKETS TO KEEP WARM.

WATER METER

HOT WATER OUT

SHUT OFF VALVE TO THE HOUSE

TO THE WATER SUPPLY

COLD WATER IN

CLEAN OUT DRAIN

TO THE SEWAGE SYSTEM

BIG FAT WASTE PIPES

EACH DRAIN HAS A TRAP TO PREVENT SMELLY SEWER GAS FROM SEEPING IN.

DRAIN VALUE

105

The River
Through Your House

Put your ear to the wall. You will hear the sounds of the river that runs through your house. You may have never thought of it as a river, but this rush of water runs through your house in much the same way as it splashes down a stream or pours over Niagara Falls. The water is governed by the same physical laws that govern the rapids that rush through the Grand Canyon. In your house this wild water is tamed by a system of pipes and gates called plumbing.

In the old days if a person needed some water in the house, he or she went to the river, pond, or well to get some and carried it back. It was heavy, awkward work, and a lot of water was lost along the way. Then somebody got the idea of letting the river run through the house. Plumbing was invented.

THE BOOK LOUSE PREFERS MOLDS BUT WILL EAT BOOKS OR PAPERS, ESPECIALLY IF THEY ARE DAMP. OF COURSE, ITS FAVORITE IS DAMP, MOLDY BOOKS.

The Source

Water from your tap can come from a lot of places. It can come from a well in your backyard, a local lake, or a river miles away. You might be drinking water from a natural spring that wells up out of the ground, or water from melted snow in the mountains. Some people in Southern California drink water from the Colorado River, which is hundreds of miles away across the dry, dusty desert. People in cities in Spain drink water that is carried by aqueducts (waterways) that were built by the Romans a couple thousand years ago. The idea of bringing the river to the door is not a new one. People have often gone to great expense to bring water to their door.

Do you know the source of your water? Ask someone. If you can't get an answer, call the local water department (the one that sends the water bills). Someone there should be able to tell you where your next drink is coming from.

Detectives On Tap

Pick a faucet in your house. Now see if you can find out the path of the pipes that bring the water gushing out of this faucet. You might start your search by looking under the sink. Then try the basement. Try putting your ear to the wall.

106

Hint: If it's hot water, the pipes will lead to the hot water heater. Do you have any idea where the hot water heater is?

If you have finished that assignment and want to try something else, trace the path of the waste water as it leaves the sink under the very same faucet.

Do you enjoy being a plumbing detective? Here are some other things to find out. Where is the main source of water to the house? Do you know how to turn it off? This can be a very handy thing to know if you're home alone when a pipe breaks.

UNDERNEATH THE SINK ARE KNOBS THAT SHUT OFF THE FAUCETS. IF YOU CAN'T FIND THEM, TRY TURNING OFF THE MAIN SOURCE TO THE HOUSE UNTIL YOU CAN GET HELP.

A Stranger-Than-Fiction Plumbing Story

You have heard about alligators in the sewers and runaway boa constrictors in the plumbing, but have you heard about birds in the toilet? Here is a story told by a plumber who plumbs for a living.

A lady called one morning and said, "Birds, they are the problem. These birds, they fly out of my toilet. They're wet and scared and make a horrible mess flapping around the bathroom."

John, the plumber, thought maybe this lady had some other kind of problem, one that a plumber couldn't fix. But conquering his reservations, he went off to see what he could do. It turned out that it was true. This lady did have birds flying out of her toilet, grackles to be exact.

Naturally, this lady had not considered looking on the roof for the source of her plumbing problem. Those vents on the roof are as much a part of the plumbing system as the pipes under the sink. The birds had found the vents a cozy place to roost because they supplied a nice draft of air. It was so comfortable that they occasionally dozed off and fell into the vent. The next thing they knew they were wet and rumpled in the toilet. The problem was solved by placing a protective screen over the vent.

The moral: It pays to know your pipes.

Hard Water

Water can be more than wet. It can be hard. Or it can be soft. Do you know if your water is hard or soft? Ask the person who does the wash at your house. Here is a way to test the local water to find out if it is hard or soft.

To do this test you will need a sample of local tap water and a sample of either rain water or distilled water for comparison. (These last two have no minerals in them.) Also you will need a little soap jelly.

1. To make soap jelly pour a little hot water over some soap shavings. Let them stand until they get soft like jelly. A little stirring will hurry them along.

2. Pour a sample of tap water into a small jar. Pour a sample of rain or distilled water into another jar.

3. Add two drops of soap jelly to each.

4. Put on the lids and shake the samples.

POUR A LITTLE HOT WATER OVER SOME SOAP SHAVINGS.

TAP WATER

DISTILLED OR RAIN WATER

SUDS ARE A SIGN OF SOFT WATER.

Lots of suds is a sign of soft water. Did you get suds in both jars? If not, you must have hard water.

Now that you know which it is, do you know why?

Hint: To solve this mystery think about what distilled water has in it that ordinary water might not. Think about what gets left behind in the kettle of boiling water. That's right, rocks. Or, more precisely, dissolved minerals. The most common ones are calcium and magnesium.

Look for the Furry Lining

Have you ever heard of a fur-lined teakettle? It's not so crazy as you might think. In fact, you might be able to find a sample of this fur in your kitchen at this very moment. Get a flashlight and have a look at the bottom of the teakettle. If it is an old kettle or if your water is really hard, you will find a layer of white minerals that is sometimes called fur or boiler scale. These minerals get into the water as it travels to your house. Find out the source of your local water supply, and you may discover the source of the lining in your teakettle.

Whirlies in the Bathtub

Did you know that the action of the earth's rotation combined with the motion of its circumnavigation around the sun may have a direct effect on your dirty bath water? Astounding, but true.

The little whirlpool that happens right around the drain when you pull the plug to empty the tub is caused by the motion of our planet Earth.

Not only that, but some scientists say this motion is exactly opposite on the other side of the globe. That's right, a kid in Australia pulls the plug on his tub and the water whirls down the drain the opposite way around.

The name of this unseen power that works on draining water is Coriolis Force.

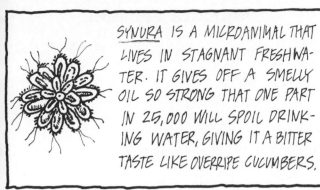

SYNURA IS A MICROANIMAL THAT LIVES IN STAGNANT FRESHWATER. IT GIVES OFF A SMELLY OIL SO STRONG THAT ONE PART IN 25,000 WILL SPOIL DRINKING WATER, GIVING IT A BITTER TASTE LIKE OVERRIPE CUCUMBERS.

Infamous Soap Curds

Were you appalled when you emptied the bathtub and saw the horrible ring? How did you get so dirty?

It might not be your fault. You could be a victim of the infamous soap curds. No, it's not a plot. It's some unfortunate bathtub chemistry that is caused by hard water. You don't like taking a bath in a tub full of chemical reactions? Relax. This is harmless chemistry.

Actually, chemistry is the reason you take a bath. Water is very good at dissolving things, especially the dirt and salt from your skin. Water is so good at dissolving things that it often streams into your bathtub with all sorts of minerals already dissolved in it. However, there are a couple of things water can't dissolve: oil and grease. That's where the soap comes in. Soap is a block of chemical reactions that melts grease. Soap makes for a happy, sudsy bath, unless the water contains lots of minerals. When soap meets minerals, the results are the icky, sticky soap curds.

To make infamous soap curds you will need to make some really hard water. Do this by dissolving one tablespoon of epsom salts in a glass of water. You can get epsom salts at the drugstore.

1. Fill a glass half-full of soapy water. Be sure to use soap, not detergent.

2. Pour some hard water into the soapy solution. Yuck, what do you see?

Hardness in water is generally caused by calcium and magnesium, dissolved in the water. These minerals are invisible until they meet up with soap.

EPSOM SALTS

POUR IN THE HARD WATER.

HOT WATER (GIVE IT A GOOD STIR.)

SUDS

HOLD IT UP TO THE LIGHT AND HAVE A LOOK.

Send Away: Water Willing

Did you know that the first complete water system had pipes that were made of fire-charred logs with holes bored in them? You can learn about this and other fascinating bits of information, including how to build a water filter and meet your water meter. All this and more is contained in a colorful comic book called "The Story of Drinking Water," starring a zippy character called Water Willing. It is free from:

American Water Works Association
6666 West Quincy Avenue
Denver, Colorado 80235

SOAP BITS

POUR IN THE SOAP. ADD ENOUGH WATER TO MAKE A PASTE.

A BEATER WILL HELP TAKE THE LUMPS OUT.

USE A STYROFOAM CUP OR A PAPER FROZEN JUICE TUBE.

PUT KNOTS IN THE ENDS OF THE STRINGS.

PEEL AWAY THE CONTAINER WHEN THE SOAP IS DRY.

Soap on a Rope

Here is a snazzy way to use those leftover bits of soap that are too small to use for washing. You can melt them down to make a big hunk that you can wear around your neck in the bathtub. You will be saving soap, and it makes a nifty present.

1. Collect at least one cupful of handsoap scraps.
2. Put them in the top of a double boiler.
3. As the water boils, the soap will melt. Stir the soap as it melts. You can add color and scent when it is completely melted.
4. Pour the soap into a form. Fill it halfway. Stick in the rope and finish filling the form with the soap.

Surface Tension

Ask your mom, your dad, anybody, "Will a piece of steel float on water?" They will probably say no. You would probably have answered no, too, but that was before you knew about surface tension, that amazing force that acts on water. Amaze your friends, amaze your relatives, amaze yourself—prove that you can actually float a piece of steel on water. Here is how:

1. Fill a saucer with water.
2. Find a razor blade or a paper clip. If you use a paper clip, bend up one end for a handle.
3. Gently place the metal piece on the surface of the water. Take care not to ripple the water. If you don't poke through the surface, the razor blade or clip will float.

BEND A PAPER CLIP TOOL OR USE YOUR FINGERS.

IT FLOATS!

TRY FLOATING:
PAPER CLIP
MESH

110

Now that you have that piece of magic mastered, are you ready to find out the reason why you, an ordinary mortal, can make metal float? You might have noticed that when the razor blade was resting on the surface of the water, it seemed to press down on the water almost as if it had a skin. The amazing truth is that water does have a skin. This skin, or surface tension, as the scientists like to call it, is the result of the hydrogen bonds that hold water together in liquid form. Along the surface these bonds stick together forming a sort of skin, skin tough enough to support a piece of metal.

Meniscus Magic

Here is another bit of science that will amaze your friends and make you the life of the party. And, if not, your mother will be impressed. All you need is a glass of water and a cork. The real wizards among you can conjure up the reason that makes this bit of magic work.

Hint: The initials are S.T.

You can add this to your list of magic tricks. Gather up an audience, a cork, and two glasses with water in them.

1. Fill one glass half-full of water.

2. Hand that glass and the cork to a member of the audience. Ask that person to float the cork on the water.

3. When the cork floats, congratulate the person and ask him or her to float the cork so it doesn't touch the sides. No fair using their hands, but the equipment on the table can be used. (You will have left the other glass with water on the table.)

4. After that person has struggled awhile, demonstrate how it is done. Pour more water into the glass with the cork in it. When it is full, carefully pour in a little extra to make a meniscus.

5. Amazing! The cork will float at the highest point of the meniscus (the curved upper surface of the liquid) without touching the sides.

POUR IN THE WATER TO MAKE A MENISCUS.

MENISCUS

YOU WILL SEE A MENISCUS WHENEVER YOU POUR WATER INTO A NARROW CONTAINER. FILL IT FULL AND YOU WILL SEE AN UPWARD BULGE. IF IT IS NOT FULL, YOU WILL NOTICE A REVERSE MENISCUS.

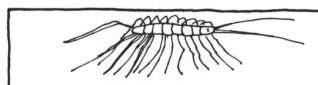

THE HOUSE CENTIPEDE IS ALSO KNOWN AS HUNDRED-FOOT. IT IS SHY AND PREFERS LIFE IN DARK DAMP SPOTS, LIKE CELLARS WHERE IT FEEDS ON INSECTS. CONSIDER THIS SMALL HARMLESS BEAST A HOUSE GUEST RATHER THAN A HOUSE PEST.

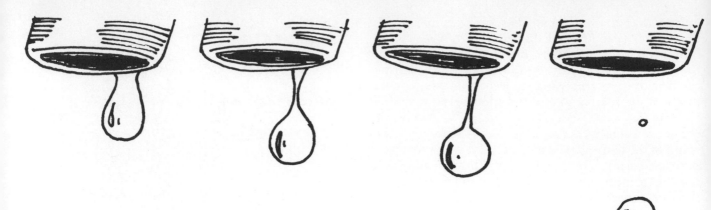

Watching Water Skin

Do you want to watch water skin in action? Take a trip to a faucet to watch some drops being formed. Drops don't just fall off the faucet. They are formed because of the tension of water across the mouth of the tap. Turn on the tap so it drips very slowly. Watch the drips. If you watch carefully, you will see that it seems as if water is made out of clear, transparent, stretchy material.

Making Water Wetter

Yes, water can be made wetter. You probably have a couple of wetting agents lurking around your house at this very moment. They also go by the names soap or detergent. These wetting agents go to work to break up the hydrogen bonds, which lessens the surface tension. If you are interested in a little action, enlist their help and watch them bust up some surface tension. While you're doing that you can think about why someone might want wetter water.

This action works incredibly fast. So you might want to try it more than once. The second time around you may have a hard time getting the razor to float. Your problem is soap. Rinse the dish again and again till all the soap is gone. Remember this test when you're rushing through the dishwashing.

1. Float a razor blade or paper clip on water. See the experiment on surface tension on page 110.

2. Make a strong soap solution with water and soap flakes or soap granules.

3. Using a straw or an eyedropper, let a little of the soap solution trickle into the water at the edge of the saucer. Don't make waves.

How long does the tension last? Is it the same for detergent solution? What happens when you stick in a corner of a bar of hand soap?

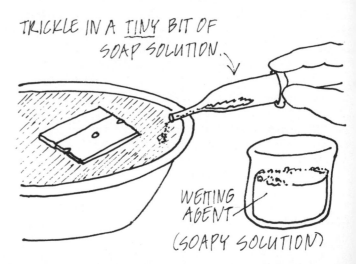

TRICKLE IN A *TINY* BIT OF SOAP SOLUTION.

WETTING AGENT

(SOAPY SOLUTION)

Soap Boat

Tired of your rubber ducky? Make a little boat that is powered by soap to keep you company in the tub. By now you should know enough about the action of water and soap to explain the science of how it works.

1. Cut a boat shape from a milk carton.
2. Make a fuel compartment in the rear of the boat with a paper punch. The rear should be open slightly.
3. You need some crumbs of hand soap that float for fuel.
4. Launch your soap boat in the bathtub. Drop a bit of soap in the fuel compartment and watch it go. Calm water is best for sailing soap boats.

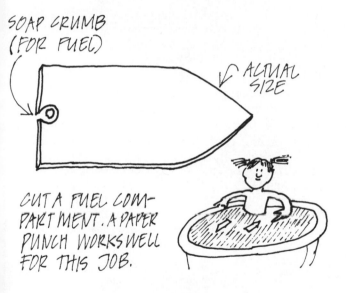

SOAP CRUMB (FOR FUEL)

ACTUAL SIZE

CUT A FUEL COMPARTMENT. A PAPER PUNCH WORKS WELL FOR THIS JOB.

Bubble Mechanics

A bubble is a bit of gas that is trapped in an envelope of fluid. When you turn on the bathtub tap full blast, you can see bubbles being formed where the water falls in. Air is being carried under the surface by the falling water. Since air is lighter than water, it floats to the top surface. As it surfaces, the skin of the water is stretched. A bubble is made when the surface tension of the water forms a thin film around a blob of air. Bubbles are born due to our old friend, surface tension.

You have no doubt noticed that when you add a bit of soap to the water, the bubbles last a lot longer. This is because the soap weakens the surface tension. The film of water becomes more elastic. The trapped air inside the bubble isn't squeezed as hard with the looser, more relaxed surface tension, so the air stays trapped inside for a longer time.

Soap bubbles can last a long time. In fact, the remains of people's wash and bubble baths are sometimes seen in streams and rivers as a soapy froth. It can take a long time for soap to break down. Detergents take even longer. Take care when you pour in the bubble bath. Use only what you need. Too much bubble bath may be making life miserable for some poor walk-on-water bug downstream.

Water Closet

Bathroom historians say that Queen Elizabeth I was one of the first people to own and operate her own flush toilet. The toilet was engineered by her nephew, who had this wondrous device installed in her country house in Richmond about 1595. Queen Elizabeth was enthusiastically flushing her water closet (toilet) into the river Thames. She, being sensitive of nose, highly recommended this newfangled device.

It wasn't until centuries later that the general population was able to follow the queen's example and install water closets at home. The first problem was that usually there was not enough water indoors to flush them. Second, there was no place to flush the waste. And third, some people saw no reason to flush at all. In those days people were accustomed to chamber pots and didn't know that sewage standing around could create all sorts of unpleasant health problems. They thought they were getting along fine just having the modern, new container for the waste.

Only after the germ theory caught on did people feel inclined to do away with wastes in an organized way. Monumental feats of engineering and cooperation built those vast networks of sewers and drains. Only in this century has it been possible for every house to hook into this disposal network, and everyone is allowed the privilege of flushing wastes away with gallons of fresh water. Now cities everywhere have the new problem of how to get these wastes out of our rivers, lakes, and oceans.

What's in Sewage?

The question you were afraid to ask. Actually, sewage contains all sorts of stuff. I know what you are thinking, but the truth is that sewage is mostly water. Only one-tenth of one percent is solid matter. Sewage is whatever is flushed from homes and businesses. It's human waste, spit, ground-up garbage, suds, chemicals. Sewage also contains wastes from industries and the waste water from street drains, plus whatever soils these drains carry into it. There is also, of course, the microlife that finds this gludge tasty.

SPICES, BREAD, BOOKS, EVEN STRYCHNINE ARE ALL FOOD FOR THE DRUGSTORE BEETLE. THEY CAN EVEN EAT THEIR WAY THROUGH TINFOIL AND LEAD. THEY LIVE IN HOMES AND WAREHOUSES.

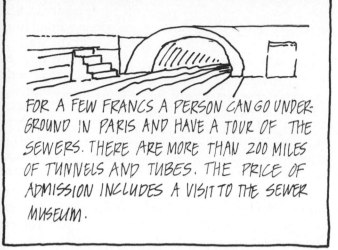

FOR A FEW FRANCS A PERSON CAN GO UNDER-GROUND IN PARIS AND HAVE A TOUR OF THE SEWERS. THERE ARE MORE THAN 200 MILES OF TUNNELS AND TUBES. THE PRICE OF ADMISSION INCLUDES A VISIT TO THE SEWER MUSEUM.

Waste Away

Squirt, rinse, flush. A blast of water and away goes all of those things nobody likes to think about. Bits of food, globs of fat, fingernail dirt, dirty wash water, the contents of the toilet bowl. A flash of water and it disappears down the tubes. Where does it go? What happens to all of the yucky stuff that gets flushed out of your life?

If you live in a town or a big city, it goes into the city sewer system. The city sewers send all waste to treatment plants where it is purified.

If you live in a rural area, it is probably flushed in-to an underground pool called a septic tank, located somewhere in your yard.

There are still places where sewage doesn't get treated at all. It gets dumped into the nearest lake or stream. If a very small amount of sewage is dumped into a rather large body of water, the local bacteria can handle it. The water doesn't necessarily get pol-luted. Unfortunately, it is sometimes a case of "out of sight, out of mind," and no one pays much attention. That attitude can result in contaminated water or a dead river.

Send Away: Captain Hydro

Holy hydrolics! It's Captain Hydro, the lovable guy who fights evil water waste. This comic adventure has a number of experiments, plus puzzles and problems to make you waterwise.

You might be able to get a free copy from your local water company. If not, send 50 cents to:

Innovative Communications
P.O. Box 23205
Pleasant Hill, California 94523

What Happens to Sewage?

Is there hope for such thoroughly contaminated water? Can it ever come clean?

The answer is yes. Sewage can be transformed into sparkling clean water. This miracle can be ac-complished with the aid of filters, chemicals, and settling tanks. Nature has come to the rescue by in-venting microlife that loves to munch on the organic wastes in water. For millions of years these tiny crea-tures have made their living by eating up organic bits in water. The result of their preferences is sparkling clean water. Sewage treatment offers these creatures free meals. When the food runs out, they die and settle to the bottom of the tank. The cleaned water moves on.

These same bacteria do their jobs whether they're in a pond, in your septic tank, or in a million-dollar sewage treatment plant.

Dry Digestors

Sanitary engineers have proposed a daring new plan for getting waste out of water. They suggest not dumping sewage wastes in water in the first place. They are proposing a new kind of waterless toilet called a dry digestor.

Are you a little nervous about living with something called a digestor? Don't worry. It's quite safe. Actually, it is a sort of collector. The digesting happens at the bottom of a pit, thanks to a lot of microlife that dines on solid waste. This microlife converts the waste into a kind of gas and dry ash. The ash is safe, sanitary stuff that can be poured on the garden to nourish your daisies.

The gas is that wonderful stuff called methane. It's the same gas that is piped to your house and burns with the reassuring blue flame. The only difference between the home-grown and the commercial kind supplied by the gas company is the source. Commercial methane gas is an antique gas produced millions of years ago by bacteria working on primal, rotting swamps and dinosaur dung.

ANY SORT OF ANIMAL WASTE WILL MAKE METHANE GAS. HOWEVER, PIG DUNG IS THE MOST POWERFUL STUFF. AN ENGLISH INVENTOR, HAROLD BATE, PUT IT THIS WAY:

"THE GREATER THE STINK, THE HIGHER THE OCTANE." HAROLD DRIVES A MACHINE CALLED A HOG MANURE MOBILE. HE SHOULD KNOW.

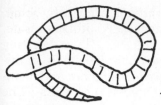

VINEGAR EELS ARE ACTUALLY LITTLE WORMS THAT FEED ON BACTERIA IN VINEGAR. YOU MIGHT SEE SOME IF YOU HOLD UP A GLASS OF CIDER VINEGAR OR HOMEMADE PICKLES TO A STRONG LIGHT. THEY ARE NOT SO COMMON THESE DAYS BECAUSE VINEGAR IS PASTEURIZED, BUT IN TIMES PAST THEY WERE THE SCOURGE OF PICKLE SHOPS.

Dead Water

In order to do their work, junk-eating microcreatures need oxygen just like we do. Most bodies of water carry along oxygen dissolved in the water. Sometimes a body of water can develop indigestion. If it gets too overloaded with wastes, its microorganisms can use up all the oxygen in the water. The bacteria suffocate, and the work of cleaning the water stops. It is a dead body of water, choked to death with wastes.

Bodies of water can be killed in other ways. Sometimes they get too much of a good thing. For instance, take phosphates. Phosphates are chemicals that are used in detergents to make them better cleaners. Phosphates are also an important plant nutrient. Every year farmers pour tons of phosphates on their fields in order to grow the biggest and best crops. These very same phosphates also do wonders making a river bloom. The plant life grows wildly and in profusion. The problem is that this new growth requires a lot of oxygen to support it. The new plants use up all the oxygen in the water, suffocating themselves along with the fish, insects, frogs, and whatever else needs oxygen. Ecologists call this type of suffocation *eutrophication*.

One way you can keep your local waters alive and well is to make sure everyone at your house uses old-fashioned soap or a low-phosphate detergent.

THESE MICROCREATURES CAN LIVE IN A GLASS OF YOUR DRINKING WATER.

SPIROCHETE EUGLENA VOLVOX

AMOEBA VORTICELLA FLAT WORM

ACTUALLY YOU NEED A MICROSCOPE TO SEE THESE TINY PLANTS AND ANIMALS. MOST LIKELY YOU WOULDN'T FIND THEM IN YOUR GLASS BECAUSE YOUR WATER SUPPLY IS TREATED WITH CHLORINE TO KILL MICROLIFE.

The Garbage Business

How long does it take your wastebasket to get full? How about the family garbage can? Have you ever thought about how big a pile your yearly garbage would make? Have you ever considered how big a pile of trash the people on your street would make in a year. How about the whole city?

It is a horrifying thought, isn't it?

If someone gave you a year's worth of garbage from your city, where would you put it? Where *does* your city put it? The truth is that most big cities have so much trash they don't know what to do with it.

We all seem to be in the business of making garbage. Maybe now is the time to think about how to make less of it. You could start by taking a good look at what's there.

American trash is said to be the best in the world. Have you visited your "waste" basket lately? Did you know that it contains the raw materials for making money and topsoil, toys, gardens, and a selection of art supplies? All free for the taking. If you feel strange about rummaging through the trash, think of the stuff in there as raw material waiting for a second chance.

Coming up are a lot of ways that you can use the stuff you find in the trash. No doubt you can think of a million more ways to have a good time with junk.

Wrapping It Up

YOU CAN WRAP WITH:
BROWN BAGS
STRIPS OF CLOTH FOR TIES, OR BITS OF YARN OR STRING
OLD MAPS
COMICS
COLORED BAGS
OLD MAGAZINES
COVER TOPS FROM OLD BOXES.

The average household collects enough paper in a year's time to bury it. One way to get rid of some of that pile of paper you collect is to wrap it around those things you are planning to give away. Scrap paper can make very respectable gift wrap. If you don't like the idea of brown-bag wrap, you can always fancy it up by printing on it.

Stick Prints

Stick printing is an ancient and simple way of making designs. It works very well for printing small patterns. All you need is a collection of different kinds of stick printers and some ink or paint.

1. Collect pencils, corks, dowels, and matches. Anything that has an end surface fit to print.
2. Dip the end in ink or paint.
3. Press it on the surface you want to print.

You can carve your own designs into the end of the stick printer with a sharp knife. Keep it simple. Be careful.

GROCER'S ITCH IS CAUSED BY TEENY CHEESE MITES WHO FEED ON CHEESE, CEREAL, AND MEAT. THEY LEAVE BEHIND A BROWN POWDER OF DEAD SKINS AND EXCREMENT THAT HAVE A SWEETISH ODOR. IN FACT, SOME CHEESES ARE NOT EATEN UNTIL THEY HAVE A BROWN CRUST THAT SOME PEOPLE SAY IS VERY TASTY.

Meat Market Prints

Here are a couple more ways to go into the printing business with junk from around the house.

You will need:

styrofoam trays (the kind meat comes wrapped in)
some cardboard
scissors
glue
paint or ink
brush
paper to print on (look in the wastebasket)

1. Cut out the design you want to print from the styrofoam. Sketch it first if you like.

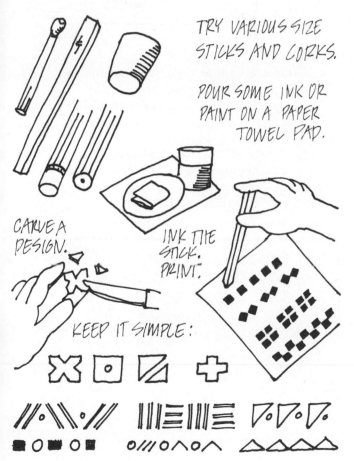

TRY VARIOUS SIZE STICKS AND CORKS.

POUR SOME INK OR PAINT ON A PAPER TOWEL PAD.

CARVE A DESIGN.

INK THE STICK. PRINT.

KEEP IT SIMPLE:

CUT OUT A SHAPE.

GLUE

CARDBOARD

2. Cut a piece of cardboard big enough to hold the design.

3. Glue the design onto the cardboard base.

4. Mix the paint or ink. It should be about as thick as cream. Roll or paint it onto the design. Don't paint the cardboard backing.

5. Press the design onto the paper.

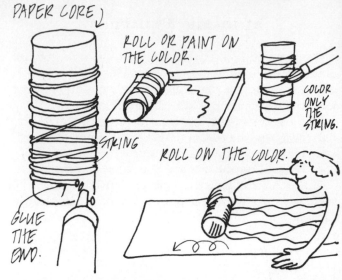

PAPER CORE

ROLL OR PAINT ON THE COLOR.

STRING

GLUE THE END.

COLOR ONLY THE STRING.

ROLL ON THE COLOR.

PAINT ONLY THE SHAPE.

PRESS THE DESIGN DOWN. CAREFULLY LIFT IT UP.

YOU CAN PRINT IT OVER AND OVER AND...

1. Wrap a length of string around the core. Hold the ends in place with glue.

2. Put paint on the wrapped string with a brush or by rolling it into a shallow dish of paint. Try to get the paint only on the string.

3. Roll the roller across the paper.

You get different designs with fat and thin string. You can also decorate the same paper with different colored runs from the same roller.

Roller Designs

Last, but not least, are the paper roll prints. These crazy line designs are made with string wrapped around the core of the toilet paper rolls. Other kinds of cores will work. Invite your friends over for a roller derby to decorate a whole stack of Christmas wrap.

BARN OWLS NEST IN HOLLOW TREES BUT SOMETIMES LIVE IN BARNS, TOWERS, AND DESERTED BUILDINGS. THE NEST OF ONE WHO HAD SETTLED IN THE SMITHSONIAN INSTITUTION IN WASHINGTON, D.C., HELD THE SKULLS OF 210 RATS, 656 HOUSE-MICE, AND 1,987 FIELD MICE. NOT BAD FOR A CITY BIRD.

120

Monster Markers

How about some giant markers that never run out of ink? When they do, you just refill them with colors you make yourself. To make these plump pens you need some roll-on deodorant bottles and paint.

1. Take the deodorant bottles apart. Wash well.
2. Mix up some poster paint. Get out all the lumps. It should be as thick as cream.
3. Pour the paint into the bottle.
4. Put the roll-on cap back on. Write away.

Don't forget to put the outer cap back on when you are finished. Collect some more bottles and fill them with different colors. Different shaped roll-ons will give you different kinds of lines.

TAKE THE BOTTLE APART:

CAP

ROLL-ON BALL

INK OR PAINT GOES HERE.

SNAP IT TOGETHER AND MARK. THINK BIG!

Diving Duck

This is a variation on the toss-and-catch games. You can make this one from a curtain ring, a piece of string, and plastic salvaged from a plastic bottle.

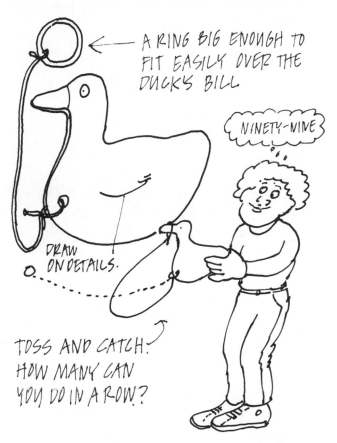

A RING BIG ENOUGH TO FIT EASILY OVER THE DUCK'S BILL

NINETY-NINE

DRAW ON DETAILS.

TOSS AND CATCH. HOW MANY CAN YOU DO IN A ROW?

1. Trace a duck onto the side of a plastic bottle. Cut out the duck.
2. Tie the ring to a piece of string about 15 inches long.
3. Attach the string to the duck. You could make a hole in the duck with a hole punch.
4. The object is to toss up the ring and catch it on the duck's bill.

Stamp Art

Famous persons, heroic events, great art, monumental inventions, wildflowers, fish, the fifty states, anniversaries, and natural wonders. These are all commemorated (remembered) on the postage stamp.

SOAK THE STAMPS.

PEEL OFF.

PRESS THEM DRY.

GLUE ON THE STAMP.

APPLY A COAT OF GLUE OVER THE STAMP.

DECORATE WITH ONE STAMP OR A WHOLE BUNCH.

OR PASTE SOME ON A SHEET OF PAPER. CUT OUT A DESIGN. GLUE IT ON.

These colorful squares that we paste on our letters are like little posters. Often they are too pretty to throw away. Here is a way to use them as decoration.

1. Collect the stamps by tearing off the entire corner of the envelope. Remember to get permission first.

2. Soak the corners in warm water for 10 minutes.

3. Pull the stamps off the paper.

4. Dry them between two layers of wax paper, pressing them with heavy books to flatten them.

5. Using a thin layer of white glue, stick the stamps onto whatever you want to decorate. Then coat the whole surface with the same glue. Let it dry.

6. Apply another coat of glue. It will dry clear, giving the stamps a shiny surface.

Spoolies

If somebody around your house does a lot of sewing, you are in luck. There are bound to be spools left when the thread runs out. Spools can be the beginnings of all sorts of good stuff. Coming up are a few ideas to get you going. A person with just a little imagination could think up more.

Spoolie Toss-Up

1. Poke a pencil or a stick through the hole in the spool so one inch of the stick protrudes above the spool. The stick needs to be about seven or eight inches long, or long enough for your hand at one end and one inch above the spool on the other.

2. Tie a string to the handle.

3. Tie a ring on the other end of the string. A curtain ring works fine.

4. Decorate the contraption. (You could make a face on the spool.)

Now you are ready to become an expert at tossing up the ring and catching it on the pointed head. Fun for the whole family.

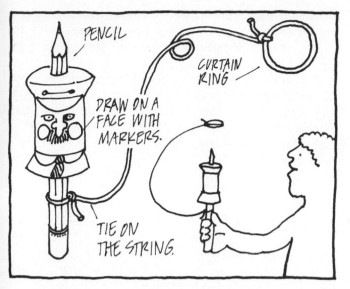

PENCIL

CURTAIN RING

DRAW ON A FACE WITH MARKERS.

TIE ON THE STRING.

Spool Top

1. Sharpen a short pencil or one end of a dowel.
2. Push it through the hole in the spool. It should fit snugly.
3. Paint the spool with bright stripes or designs.
4. When it is dry, take it out for a spin. Twirl it between your thumb and forefinger.

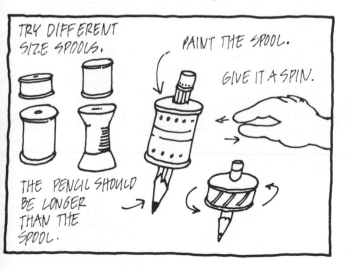

TRY DIFFERENT SIZE SPOOLS.

PAINT THE SPOOL.

GIVE IT A SPIN.

THE PENCIL SHOULD BE LONGER THAN THE SPOOL.

Spool Man from Outer Space

1. Glue two spools together. Then glue a wooden bead on top for the head.
2. Paint it to look like a space person.
3. Make a parachute for the spool man with a bandanna and four lengths of string about 18 inches long. (Tie them together like in the picture.)
4. Tie the parachute around the spool man's neck.
5. To launch him roll up the chute, take him outside, and throw him as high into the air as you can. His chute will open, and he will float down from space.

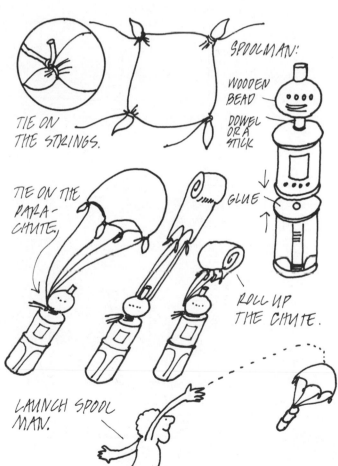

TIE ON THE STRINGS.

SPOOLMAN:

WOODEN BEAD

DOWEL OR A STICK

GLUE

TIE ON THE PARACHUTE.

ROLL UP THE CHUTE.

LAUNCH SPOOL MAN.

Cereal Box Beasts

When most people look inside a box, they are trying to find out if there are enough corn flakes left inside for breakfast. However, an ace recycler would also notice that the inside of a lot of boxes have some real possibilities. Once you turn them inside out, you have a couple of sheets of medium-weight cardboard for all sorts of art projects. Choose boxes that are clean and white inside. Make sure that they are empty before you take the scissors to them.

1. Cut off the box bottom and top. Then split open the side carefully.

2. Cut out some animals according to the patterns, or make up some of your own.

3. Fold the animals into shape or slide their parts into position.

4. Paint your menagerie.

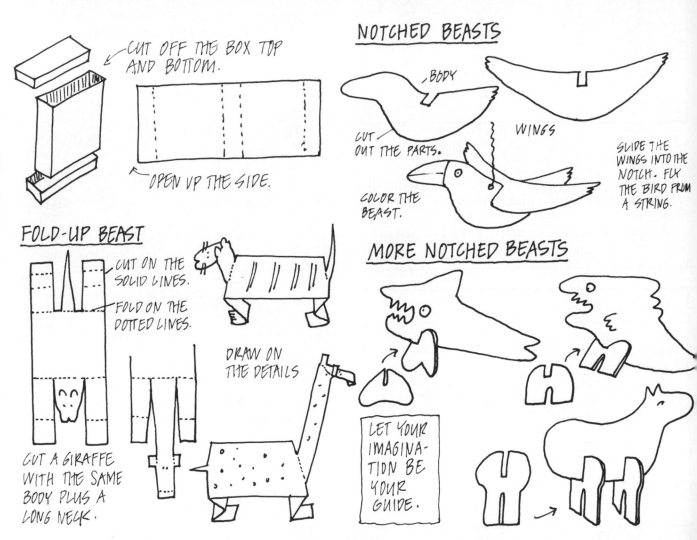

CUT OFF THE BOX TOP AND BOTTOM.

OPEN UP THE SIDE.

NOTCHED BEASTS

BODY

CUT OUT THE PARTS.

WINGS

COLOR THE BEAST.

SLIDE THE WINGS INTO THE NOTCH. FLY THE BIRD FROM A STRING.

FOLD-UP BEAST

CUT ON THE SOLID LINES.

FOLD ON THE DOTTED LINES.

DRAW ON THE DETAILS

CUT A GIRAFFE WITH THE SAME BODY PLUS A LONG NECK.

MORE NOTCHED BEASTS

LET YOUR IMAGINATION BE YOUR GUIDE.

Bleach Bottle Jai Alai

THE SCOOPS

CUT HERE

HOLD IT LIKE THIS.

BALL (AN OLD TENNIS BALL IS GOOD.)

Jai Alai (high lie) is a fast-moving game played by professionals in Spain and Mexico. Matches take place at night before lively audiences that bet on the results.

You can play a version of this game with some junk from around the house.

Get ready:

1. Cut out a pair of scoops from plastic bleach bottles—either the quart or half-gallon size will work.

2. Find a ball that you can catch in your scoop that will roll out easily. An old tennis ball will do fine.

To play:

1. Opponents stand opposite each other. One person starts off by tossing the ball to the other person.

2. The opposite player catches it in his or her scoop and slings it back. Play continues until somebody misses. A miss counts as one point for the opposite side.

The Forces

Along with all the wind currents, microclimate, plant life, chemical reactions, and wildlife that you can see, or can almost see, there are some other things happening in your house. Some obvious, some strange and mysterious, and some that might never have occurred to you. The physical world operates on many levels. Parts of it are at work in your living room right now. The forces are with you.

The Second Law Cleans House

No! You can't go anywhere until you clean up your room!

How many times have you heard that one? No matter how hard you try your room is always a mess. Your skateboard always ends up on the steps. Your T-shirts always collect in a heap in the corner. Your shoes always tangle themselves in a pile on the closet floor. The dirty clothes pile up with single socks, each of a different color. The overdue library books can never be found when it's time for the trip to the library. Where do the fat, fluffy hunks of dust come from? You surely didn't put them under your bed. You don't remember eating in bed, so how did the cookie crumbs get there? Who took your quarter that you put in the fish bowl for safekeeping? And maybe you did sort of forget to take that half cup of cold hot cocoa back to the kitchen, but you don't know how the ants found it under the bed.

OK, so your room is a mess. You are the first to admit it, but there is no use cleaning it up. It will just get dirty again. It happens every time. It's not your fault.

It seems that there is some powerful force bent on messing up your room. In fact there is. Scientists believe that things tend to go from order to disorder. They have even given a name to this phenomenon. They call it the Second Law of Thermodynamics.

SUPPOSE YOU HAD A BOX LIKE THIS AND YOU PUT BLACK MARBLES ON ONE SIDE AND WHITE ONES ON THE OTHER SIDE...

TAKE OFF THE LID. JUST AS YOU THOUGHT... DISORDER. AND IT HAPPENS EVERY TIME.

PUT THE LID ON AND GIVE IT A GOOD SHAKE.

You can see this law in operation all over the place, for instance, in the kitchen when your mom is making *garlic pie*. (Doesn't your mom make garlic pie?) The smell starts in the kitchen in a really strong concentrated form and gradually spreads all over the house. When you watch a sky writer, first the letters are readable, then they break up and blow all over the sky rather quickly. They get so disordered that you can hardly read them.

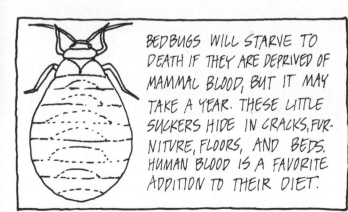

BEDBUGS WILL STARVE TO DEATH IF THEY ARE DEPRIVED OF MAMMAL BLOOD, BUT IT MAY TAKE A YEAR. THESE LITTLE SUCKERS HIDE IN CRACKS, FURNITURE, FLOORS, AND BEDS. HUMAN BLOOD IS A FAVORITE ADDITION TO THEIR DIET.

The Second Law seems to be operating in your room where things move from order to disorder with the greatest of ease. So when your mom gets mad about your messy room, you could try explaining the Second Law to her. (Then get ready to clean it up anyway — real fast.)

Under the Weather

Have you ever noticed that you feel dumb on some days? Every so often do you have a day when you can't seem to do anything right? You forget your homework, lose your sweater, and fall asleep during math class. And you love math.

It might not be all your fault. Maybe you can blame the weather. Scientists are beginning to find out that changes in the air make changes in your mental attitude and attention.

In factories it has been discovered that accidents happen more often when the temperature goes over 24 degrees centigrade or falls below 12 degrees centigrade.

126

Teachers know that kids in classrooms get into more trouble on days with high temperature and high humidity. Not only that but on low-barometer days (when the atmospheric pressure dips) it seems that there are more traffic accidents, more animals taken to dog pounds, more things left on buses, and more mistakes made in offices.

No one knows exactly why this happens. Some scientists think that the increased electrical activity in the atmosphere might somehow affect the electrical activity in our brains, like a kind of static interference.

The Weather Gets to You

Two groups of school kids were tested for their reactions to climate. One group was put in a room with the temperature and humidity carefully controlled. The other kids were left in ordinary classrooms. Their school progress was tested after several weeks. Kids in the climate-controlled room learned better and made fewer errors in their tests. The groups were switched. Same results: the kids in the climate-controlled room did better. Differences were greatest during the time air conditioning was needed. Warmth was the hardest condition to deal with.

Singing in the Shower

Why is it that people are inclined to sing in the shower, but hardly anybody sings in the bathtub? There may be a scientific explanation.

The water falling in a shower leaves the air charged with a rather large electric field of negatively charged particles. These air particles, or ions, seem to have a happy effect on human behavior. It is possible that this electric field makes you feel happy enough to want to sing.

A similar condition exists around waterfalls. People will drive or walk a long way to visit a waterfall. Some of the great resorts of the world are situated at waterfalls. If you are a keen observer of people, you will notice that even at a local lake people will often pause to watch water spill over a dam a few feet high. It may not be much to look at, but the splashing seems to attract people.

Wild Electricity

Anybody who has ever shuffled across a rug and reached out for a doorknob on a dry day knows that there is electricity loose in the house. They have had the shocking experience of a spark jumping between them and a metal doorknob. If you aren't expecting it, this spark of wild electricity can be quite a surprise.

Of course, wild electricity doesn't hide in rugs or on door handles waiting to leap out at you when you least expect it. It is quite predictable once you understand how it works.

To understand electricity you have to get down to basics. You have to know something about the atom and the particles of stuff that make up an atom.

One way to think about an atom is to picture it as a little solar system. In the center is the nucleus, which has a positive electrical charge. Circling this positive nucleus are rings of electrons that have a negative charge. The positive and negative charges are important in holding the atom together.

Some atoms have electrons that are tightly locked into position. Others have electrons that are loosely held and easily lost.

These loosely held electrons are easily attracted to positively charged surfaces. All it takes is the right material and a little rubbing to collect a lot of them. When that happens, the surface builds up a strong negative charge. Loose electrons are a fickle bunch. They will jump off the surface where they have collected whenever the oppositely charged surface comes along.

When you shuffle across a rug, you are collecting electrons on the soles of your shoes. By the time you get to the door you're so negatively charged that the electrons literally leap off your hand to the positive knob.

Shocking, isn't it?

Electron Glue

Up against the wall with electron forces. You can stick paper cutouts to the wall by charging them with a woolen cloth. You'll know when your forces are weakening. Your cutouts will come crashing down.

CUT OUT SOME PAPER CREATURES.

RUB A PENCIL OVER THE CUTOUTS SEVERAL TIMES IN THE SAME DIRECTION.

Note: You can collect electrons by rubbing things with certain materials. Wool, hair, fur, and silk are all materials that pick up a charge.

1. Cut some creatures out of paper. You can use the newspaper if you don't mind the print.

2. Rub a pencil over the cutouts several times in the same direction to work up some static electricity. Rubbing a wool cloth over the cutouts will also work.

3. Press them to the wall. If you have done a good job making static electricity, they will stick to the wall.

PRESS THEM TO THE WALL

More Static Magic

Here are some more things that you can do to test the power of static electricity. If you can find a glass or plastic wand and you have a talent for showing off, you can pass yourself off as a magician.

1. Find a glass rod or a plastic wand. The handle of a flyswatter will work well.

2. Rub the wand with a wool cloth to charge it with static electricity.

3. Amaze your friends with your wand's ability to pick up paper cutouts, toothpicks, and bits of tinsel. Of course, part of the magic is how well you present the trick. Try to convince your audience that the magic is in the wand and not in the cloth.

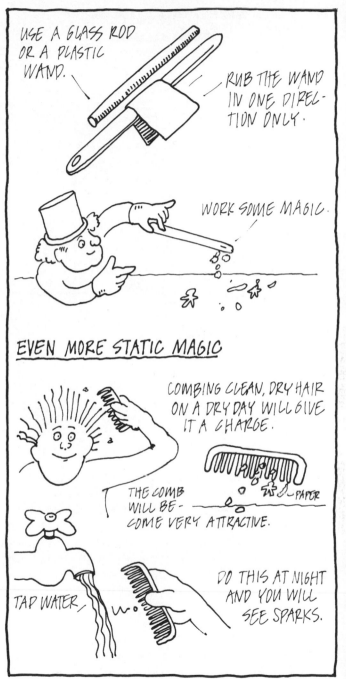

USE A GLASS ROD OR A PLASTIC WAND.

RUB THE WAND IN ONE DIRECTION ONLY.

WORK SOME MAGIC.

EVEN MORE STATIC MAGIC

COMBING CLEAN, DRY HAIR ON A DRY DAY WILL GIVE IT A CHARGE.

THE COMB WILL BECOME VERY ATTRACTIVE.

PAPER

TAP WATER

DO THIS AT NIGHT AND YOU WILL SEE SPARKS.

Electromagnetic Radiation

Passing through your room are all sorts of waves. Some of them you can see. They are the light waves. These are the waves that we know as visible light. Visible light is only a thin slice of the wide range of waves that fly through our atmosphere.

Our space is constantly being bombarded with all sorts of waves. There are radio waves, TV waves, shortwave radio waves like the sort used by the CB fans, not to mention microwaves, X-rays, and cosmic rays.

It's just as well we can't sense these waves. The noise from the dozens of different waves in the radio category alone would be enough to drive us all crazy.

More About Waves

Your natural sensory equipment can receive a few waves on either side of the thin band of light rays. One is the infrared ray. The nerve sensors that are placed all over our skin feel infrared rays as heat.

Another is the ultraviolet wave. These we can't feel until we have had too many. Ultraviolet waves are the ones that cause us to sunburn. These high-energy waves are capable of killing cells, both human skin cells and bacteria in the air. However, you are safe inside the house. Glass screens most of the ultraviolet waves and lets in only visible waves.

Special equipment is needed to receive and detect other kinds of waves. Radios can catch some waves moving through your house. TV receives waves of another length.

Solar Interference

Sometimes when you turn on the radio, all you get is a lot of electronic hisses. Before you give the old radio a whack you might find out if there have been any solar flares. All that static and noise might be caused by activity on the sun's surface.

Every once in a while the sun's surface explodes into what is called a solar flare. This explosion of solar gas is sent thousands of miles into space. Some of this energy is pointed in the earth's direction. We get a shower of particles that is seen as the aurora borealis, or the northern lights. This rain of solar energy plays havoc with the radio waves. The result is static racket when you tune into your favorite rock 'n' roll.

Winds in the House?

Cigarette smoke drifts around the room in streams that look a lot like rivers. Doors sometimes shut themselves mysteriously. Standing next to a big window on a cold day in a warm house you will notice the tiniest draft. These things are not your imagination. The air in your house is constantly on the move. These microbreezes blow for the same reasons and in much the same way that the big winds blow outside your house. You can learn a lot about outdoor weather by studying the indoor winds.

One of the hardest things about studying air is that you can't get your hands on it. And you can't smell or see it, unless it is carrying some pretty unsavory particles. Most of the time you forget that it is there.

TINY BITS CALLED POLLEN GRAINS ARE SENT INTO THE AIR IN SEARCH OF FEMALE FLOWERS. AT CERTAIN TIMES OF THE YEAR ZILLIONS OF POLLEN GRAINS ARE BLOWN ABOUT BY WINDS. THEY GIVE LOTS OF PEOPLE RED EYES, RUNNY NOSES, AND A CASE OF THE SNEEZES — INDOORS — AND OUT.

PIN-HEAD

RAG-WEED POLLEN

If you have ever tried to walk into a strong wind, you quickly became aware of the presence of air. And if you have ever gotten a hole in your bicycle tire, you were reminded of air's absence.

What you may not know is that even though it remains stubbornly invisible, air goes through a lot of changes. These changes make for big differences in our climate, indoors and out.

Air Streams

Winds are streams of air molecules that are rushing around. Why do air molecules rush around? Well, they are sometimes under a lot of pressure. (Example: You can create a little wind by putting pressure on your cheeks. First fill your mouth full of air. Now put some pressure on your cheeks. The result, unless you have inhumanly strong lips, is a blast of air between your lips. A little wind.) Winds come about because air molecules rush from areas of high pressure to areas of low pressure.

The next question is where does all that pressure come from? Areas of high pressure and low pressure are created by differences in temperature. Air, like any gas, is made up of atoms and molecules that fly about freely bumping into one another and into the walls of whatever contains them. When the molecules of air are heated up, they get excited. They fly about faster and bump into themselves and their container more often and with more force. We see these changes in two ways: as the heat (and pressure) increases, the gas presses against its container with more force and expands (takes up more space). It also rises.

Hot Meets Cold

WHEN A LIGHT IS ON, IT GIVES OFF HEAT. YOU CAN SEE HOT AIR STREAMS RISING FROM THE LAMP.

If you could put some hot air next to some cold air, you would get some action. The hot air, in its fast-flying frenzy, would expand into the cold. The cool air would sink to the bottom of the container because it is denser. (Its atoms are closer together.) The hot air would rise to the top because it is lighter. You would have created a little wind.

Uneven heating of the earth's air layer causes hot pools of air to rush into cold layers. Wind is created until the temperatures are equalized. These motions of molecules can happen on the planetary scale or under a lamp in the kitchen, wherever hot and cold atoms chance to meet.

BARN SWALLOWS LIKE TO NEST UNDER ROOFS OR THE EAVES OF BUILDINGS. THEY CATCH ALL THEIR FOOD IN FLIGHT AND EAT A LOT OF MOSQUITOES AND FLIES.

A Breezy Quiz

1. Why do your feet get cold when you open the refrigerator door?

2. When you open the oven door to check a batch of baking cookies, why do you get blasted in the face with a lot of hot air?

3. Why does hot, humid air come tumbling out of the bathroom when you open the door after a long, hot shower?

4. On what kinds of days will the front door slam? Why is it harder to slam a door in winter?

5. Why do you get a wind when you open the door on a winter day, but no wind on a spring day?

6. Say you leave the door open on a cold day and your mother yells at you to close it. Is she mad at you because the heat is going out or because the cold is getting in?

7. Why do the tall upright freezer cases in markets have doors on them and low ones don't?

Note: The answers are on page 134.

Breaking the News

You can impress your friends with your magical powers or your knowledge of physics with this trick. You will impress yourself that air is indeed there and that air can be a real drag.

1. Find a flat stick about a yard long that nobody minds if you break.

2. Set it on a table with about half the length of it sticking over the edge.

3. Spread a sheet of newspaper over the yardstick. Make sure it is very flat with no air spaces between it and the table.

4. Here is the part where you need everyone's attention while you perform this amazing feat. With one sure, swift blow give the stick a karate chop. If you do it right, the pressure of the paper will hold the stick down while you break it in half. Applause.

No applause? Then you need a bit of practice with your karate chop.

SET THE STICK ON THE TABLE WITH HALF OF IT STICKING OVER THE EDGE.

SMOOTH OUT ALL THE AIR SPACES BETWEEN THE PAPER AND THE TABLE.

GIVE THE STICK A GOOD WHACK. YOU MIGHT HAVE TO PRACTICE A BIT TO LEARN HOW TO MAKE A CLEAN BREAK.

133

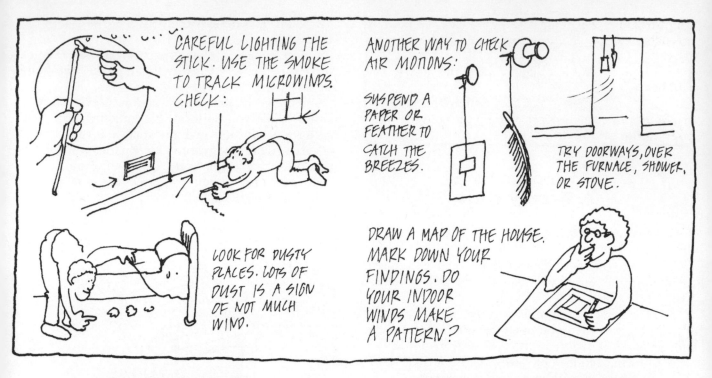

Wind Tracing

You might think about mapping the way the wind blows inside your house. Make a drawing of the floor plan of your house. You can indicate where the doors and windows are. Draw in the heater, the fireplace, and the air conditioner if you have them. Trace the winds around your house with a stick of incense. The long kind that you can hold on one end works best. The smoke from the slowly burning stick will give you some clues as to which way the wind blows.

Look for winds wherever there is a heat source and in passageways where cool air may meet up with air from a warmer part of the house.

Check the windows and doors for little breezes around the edges. How about the crack under the front door? Can you find any dead air spaces (areas where the air doesn't move) in your house? Where are the prevailing winds?

Answers to Breezy Quiz

1. When you open the refrigerator, the heavy cold air falls to the floor. The result is cold toes, and a hot refrigerator if you stand there long enough.

2. A hot oven is really a little room full of excited air molecules. When you open the door, they fly out and rise. If you are in the way, you will get blasted.

3. It is similar to opening the oven door, except you can see the hot air from the shower because of the water droplets in it.

4. Doors slam on days when the temperature outside is the same as the temperature inside. On cold days when you open the door, the heat rushes outside into the cold air. When you close the door, the rushing air acts as a cushion, preventing the door from slamming.

5. On a spring or autumn day the temperature outside is the same as the temperature inside. There

is no stream of warm air rushing outside, so there is no cushion effect. The door slams shut with a normal shove.

6. Think about it. Then reread the answer to number 4.

7. Cold air lies like a blanket in a horizontal freezer. An upright needs doors to keep the cold air from pouring out on the floor.

Wind Darts

Every kid who has blown out birthday candles knows that it's easy to make a little wind by making a high pressure area inside your cheeks and letting it go. With a little practice you can direct these jet streams and be a winner at this fascinating game called wind darts. Before long folks might be calling you a windbag.

1. You need to find some sanitary straws (the kind that come wrapped in paper) to make the darts.

2. To make a dart, push off the paper wrapper, cut it in half, and twist one end shut.

3. To shoot the dart, put the paper cover on one end of the straw, aim, and puff some air through the other end.

4. When you have practiced a little, make a cardboard target and challenge a friend to a wind dart shooting contest.

TWIST THE END.

SLIP THE DART ON THE STRAW AND PUFF!

Bernoulli Balance

PUT THE BALL INTO THE IN-VISIBLE WALL. MAGIC!

ORDINARY PING-PONG BALL

SET UP THE VACUUM HOSE. YOU MIGHT TRY MAKING A BOX HOLDER. →

Vacuum cleaners are wind-making machines in reverse. They suck instead of blow. If you have a vacuum cleaner that has a hose that you can remove and connect to the exhaust, you can use it to balance a ball on a stream of wind.

The wind in this trick makes an invisible wall that holds the ball in place.

1. Set up the vacuum cleaner so that it blows rather than sucks. (On most vacuum cleaners this is accomplished by attaching the hose to the exhaust outlet.)

2. Prop up the air hose so that it points toward the ceiling.

3. Place a ping-pong ball in the air stream.

4. Invite your friends in to impress them with your knowledge of physics.

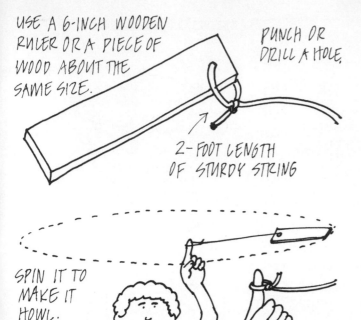

USE A 6-INCH WOODEN RULER OR A PIECE OF WOOD ABOUT THE SAME SIZE.

PUNCH OR DRILL A HOLE.

2-FOOT LENGTH OF STURDY STRING

SPIN IT TO MAKE IT HOWL.

KNOT THE STRING AROUND YOUR FINGER FOR SAFTEY.

Howling Winds, Whistling Breezes

Have you ever lain in bed and listened to the sound of the wind howling outside your window or heard a breeze whistle through your house. You might have wondered how the wind can make such spooky sounds. Here is an easy-to-make toy that will answer that question with howling success.

The secret of this toy is a long string that is attached to a weight. There are many ways to make it, each of which will give you a different noise.

1. Knot a string around the end of a flat piece of wood such as a small ruler.

2. To make your contraption howl, spin it around your head as fast as you can. Be careful you don't hit anything, or anyone.

When strings vibrate they make sounds. The wind blowing past telephone lines causes them to vibrate and make sounds. This toy reverses the action. You make the wind and noises.

Mapping Microclimate

If you were a person about an inch tall, where in your house do you think you would feel the most at home. What sort of a microclimate would you choose? In your house where is: the hottest spot? the sunniest space? the dampest place? the coldest corner?

How many microclimates can you find in your house? You probably have some suspicions about where these spots are. A thermometer and a light meter (if you have one) will help confirm your suspicions. Also, evidence of wildlife tells you a lot about the different climates in the house. For instance, wood lice marching across the living room rug means there is damp wood somewhere, no matter how much you would like to pretend otherwise.

Climate is a special weather condition that is basically a combination of three things: heat, light, and humidity (water in the air). There are a lot of different combinations. It can be damp and cool (as in a fern forest) or hot and humid (as in Washington, D.C., in the summer). These conditions can be with sun or without.

Living things are generally suited to live in one climate or another. If they are put in the wrong place, they sometimes struggle along; or if they are really misfits for the place, they just won't survive. Boston ferns are not really house plants. They are used to living on forest floors in the cool damp. They hate sunny windows, so if you want a Boston fern to move into your house and feel at home, you had better find a proper microclimate for it.

MAPPING MICROCLIMATE

USE A ROOM THERMOMETER TO FIND THE HOT SPOTS IN YOUR HOUSE. YOU MIGHT NEED TO MAKE A HOLDER.

WILDLIFE CAN GIVE YOU CLUES ABOUT MICROCLIMATE.

CHECK OUT THE TEMPERATURE AT DIFFERENT ALTITUDES IN YOUR ROOM.

MOLDS ARE A SURE SIGN OF DAMPNESS. SOFT WOOD (TEST IT WITH YOUR FINGERNAIL) IS A SIGN OF ROT, ALSO A SIGN OF DAMPNESS.

WILTED INDOOR PLANTS AND CHAPPED LIPS ARE A SIGN OF DRYNESS.

SURE IS DARK IN THIS CLOSET.

USE A LIGHT METER TO MEASURE THE AMOUNT OF LIGHT. IF YOU CAN'T BORROW ONE, JUST USE YOUR EYES.

IF YOU LIKE DRAWING MAPS, MAKE ONE OF YOUR HOUSE. SHOW THE WETTEST, COLDEST, AND DRIEST MICROCLIMATES. DON'T FORGET TO CHECK THE ATTIC, UNDER THE SINK, THE STOVE TOP, AND IN THE BATHROOM.

Send Away: World in a Bottle

How about a little tropical rain forest for a corner of your room? You can make a bottle garden (terrarium) that will act just like a miniature steaming jungle. You can watch the rain run down the inside of the jar. The best part about this kind of garden is that it doesn't need much care because it creates its own climate inside the bottle.

You can get instructions on how to make a terrarium from the Massachusetts Audubon Society. Write and ask for teaching sheet 061 called "How to Make a Terrarium." It costs 60 cents from:

Massachusetts Audubon Society
Public Information Office
Lincoln, Massachusetts 01773

A Breath of Fresh Air

In all sorts of weather folks flee the stuffy indoors for a breath of fresh air. While the air outdoors may not be fresh, it is at least different from a close room crowded with smells. Have you ever wondered just what it is that makes a smell?

The molecules of a substance are constantly exchanging with their outside environment. Or more simply, they are breaking off and floating away into space. A smell happens when tiny particles of a thing get inside your nose. Your nose is specially equipped with sensors to let you know that these particles are present. In other words, these particles smell. Or more correctly, your nose "tastes" them and identifies them as smells.

Of course, some things smell a lot more than others. The more smell, the more molecules are being lost. Perfumes and ammonia are famous for their smells. You can bet they are throwing off a lot of particles. On the other hand, a hunk of steel doesn't have much of a smell, although rusty iron has more. Iron is more stable and hangs on to its molecules.

SUPPOSE YOUR NOSE COULD SMELL MARBLES. THEN IT COULD SENSE ONE MARBLE OF MERCAPTAN IN A SUPERMARKET FILLED WITH MARBLES.

Certain Smells

Have you ever noticed that your best friend's house smells different from your own? It has a different smell from your grandmother's house, which is quite unlike your piano teacher's house. Take a minute to see if you can describe the way these places smell. Do you know any houses you hate the smell of? Got any idea what it is you don't like?

While humans do not have a nose that is as sensitive as a German shepherd's, our noses are pretty darn good. Mercaptan is the chemical name of the famous skunk smell. The human nose can pick up this scent in dilutions as fantastically weak as 1 part in 30,000,000,000.

One-Track Nose

The reason that houses seem to have a particular smell is that our noses can smell only one thing at a time, unlike our eyes that can see several colors at a time. In a sense you could say that we smell in black and white, as opposed to smelling in color. A number of smells combine to make up one sensation, like the smell of a house or a fish market or a locker room or a bus station.

Now that you are armed with that bit of knowledge, perhaps you will be able to figure out what it is that gives your grandma's house that peculiar scent. Maybe it's the furniture polish and the dust combined with her fondness for Brussels sprouts and cooked cabbage. Does your best friend have a new baby brother or sister? They can really smell up a house with diapers and talcum powder. Maybe your best friend always forgets to take out the kitty litter box and leaves the lids off the model airplane glue. Or perhaps you know someone who always has a bouquet of freshly cut flowers in the living room, giving the house a fresh, outdoorsy smell. Houses smell for a reason. Do some nasal research to find out what's at the bottom of those smells.

SOMETIMES SMELLS CAN BE CLUES TO THE KIND OF WILDLIFE LIVING IN A HOUSE. MOLDS, MICE, AND ROACHES EACH HAVE A SPECIAL SCENT.

139

Orange Oil Wells

Oranges have a wonderful smell. The skin of an orange is covered with little pits that are packed with an aromatic oil. You can see them with your eyes, but you can see these miniature oil wells better with a magnifier. When you peel an orange, you can see the oil glands breaking and squirting this oil as a fine mist into the air.

Oranges are not the only plants with oils that smell good. The underside of a fresh peppermint leaf has a lot of little glands filled with oil. Dill, rosemary, sage, and savory contain oils that fly up your nose. Evergreen Christmas trees have a delightful smell.

Why do plants go to so much trouble to smell?

GIVE A SLICE OF ORANGE PEEL A SQUEEZE AND WATCH THE OIL EXPLOSION.

OIL WELLS

MANY LEAVES SUCH AS MINT, SAGE, AND THYME HAVE OIL GLANDS.

CROSS SECTION OF A CARROT SEED

OIL TUBE

AROMATIC SEEDS LIKE DILL, CARAWAY, AND FENNEL CONTAIN OIL TUBES CALLED AKENES.

Invisible Smells

WELL, IF THAT'S SCIENCE, I THINK IT STINKS!

Everyone's house smells but yours, right? Wrong. If you don't believe it, ask a friend. Your friend will have noticed the scent of *your* house, but you will have a hard time convincing your friend that his or her house has any smell. Noses don't notice their everyday surroundings. No, your nose is not falling down on the job. It is working just fine. Your brain takes no notice of the same, normal, everyday smells. It can get used to new smells in just a few days. You can prove it to yourself.

You will need several days for this experiment and some sort of smelly substance that you can wear. Try your dad's shaving lotion or your mother's perfume. Give yourself a good splash of the stuff in the morning. Do it each day for a week. How many times do you notice that you have it on the first day? The second? The third? How many times do your friends notice each day?

140

Familiar Sounds

What is the most familiar sound at your house? A dog barking? The TV? The sound of traffic? Birds singing? The neighbors fighting? The little kid next door crying? Music on the radio? The sound of your sister practicing the tuba?

Wherever you live there are some familiar sounds. Wherever you live there is also noise. Noise is made up of sounds that you could do without.

Sound

Sound is interesting stuff. Actually it is more like energy than stuff. Remember that we live here at the bottom of an ocean of air. Down here the air is pretty thick, and some of it is always pressing against us. Sounds are what happen when vibrations pass through this body of air.

Your ears are nothing more than tightly stretched patches of skin at the end of tunnels. These tunnels are attached to funnels on each side of your head. The funnels collect sound vibrations, which are sent down to drums where they are converted into nerve impulses. These impulses travel to the brain. The brain makes sense of them.

THE ENGINES OF SLOW-FLYING PLANES CAN MAKE ENOUGH NOISE VIBRATIONS TO RATTLE A WINDOW.

BUT THEY ARE MILD COMPARED TO THE BIG BOOMS CAUSED BY FAST-FLYING SUPER-SONIC PLANES.

Shake, Rattle, and Roll

Every once in a while your house shakes, and the windows rattle and leap around in their frames. If you ask people why, they usually say that it was a sonic boom. If you ask them to explain a sonic boom, they will say it was made by a plane. Ask them how this happens, and they will probably send you to the encyclopedia.

When a plane flies, it creates shock waves as it moves ahead in the air, a little like waves on the water. When a plane moves slower than the speed of sound (760 mph), its own pressure waves clear a path for it. However, when a plane flies faster than the speed of sound, the pressure disturbances (sounds) it makes never catch up with it. The plane has to plow through the air and push it aside as it moves along. This head-on collision with air makes a tremendous crashing noise. It sets up a gigantic shock wave that travels down to earth. The plane trails this shocking noise after it as it flies by, rattling windows, cracking plaster, and upsetting any animal life with ears.

Nasty Noises

The roar, whir, and whine of noise around your house can actually affect your health. Sounds can make you tense, grouchy, irritable, and inattentive. Did you know that sounds can raise your blood pressure? And they can give you a headache and an upset stomach. Sounds can drive you to distraction. Did you know that most accidents at home happen in the bathroom and the kitchen, rooms where there is the most noise.

Sounds are measured in decibels. Here is a quickie decibel survey to give you an idea of the level of the sounds around your house.

DECIBELS	SOUND	DECIBELS	BODY RESPONSE
0	BARELY HEARD SOUND		
10	NORMAL BREATHING		
20	RUSTLING LEAVES		
		30–40	LOUD ENOUGH TO GET YOUR ATTENTION — A DISTRACTING SOUND
		50	ANNOYANCE BEGINS
60	TWO-PERSON CONVERSATION		
75	TELEVISION	70	YOUR BLOOD PRESSURE RISES, ARTERIES SHRINK, BLOOD SUPPLY TO THE HEART LESSENS
78	RINGING TELEPHONE		
84	VACUUM CLEANER		YOU MAKE MISTAKES, CONCENTRATION IS DIFFICULT
100	GARBAGE DISPOSAL		
		140	VERY PAINFUL TO THE EARS

Good Vibes Box

REMOVE THE FLAPS.

TAKE OFF THE CELLOPHANE.

YOU CAN SEE THE VIBRATIONS.

Musical instruments are nothing more than vibration-making machines. The music part is a matter of taste. What is music to some ears is noise to others. Here is a simple machine you can make. You will see and hear the vibrations it makes. You decide if it's music.

1. You will need a box like the ones cough drops or square pieces of gum come in.
2. Remove the flaps from one end of the box.
3. Put your lips to that end and blow.

Silence

Have you ever been in a quiet place? A place so quiet that all you could hear was the wind in the trees or the sounds of the grasshoppers? How about a place so quiet that all you could hear was your own heartbeat? It seems that no matter how quiet it is, we can always hear noise of one kind or another.

Usually you don't notice the noise because your mind puts a damper on the sounds you don't want to hear. Some of the most annoying sounds are not the really loud jangling ones, but sounds that get in the way—the rustle of somebody opening a candy wrapper in a movie theater, or a truck on the street that interrupts a conversation.

Noises can sometimes get you down, even if you aren't really aware of them. It is interesting to notice how noisy your world is. Find the quietest spot at your house. How many noises can you hear from there? Can you close it off to make it even quieter? Bet you can't find a place that is really silent.

Inside and the Great Out There

It is hard to believe that what you do in the privacy of your own home can have a worldwide impact. But it can.

For instance, the innocent tuna fish sandwich that you had for lunch may have been responsible for killing some dolphins. That's because tuna fishermen trap tuna in nets that sometimes also catch dolphins. The dolphins often drown before they are set free from the nets.

Expensive perfumes sometimes have bits of whale in them. Certain parts of the whale are prized for their smell and preservative qualities. Other parts of the whale are melted down into oil. People squirt melted whales onto their machines. In fact, whales have become so useful around the house that they are fast becoming extinct in the ocean.

The old can of air freshener with the pushbutton control is under suspicion for more than getting rid of bad smells. It seems to be getting rid of the ozone layer in the atmosphere, the layer that protects our hides from the deadly ultraviolet rays of the sun. Ultraviolet rays kill living tissue such as skin.

How can you keep from committing murder or suicide every time you turn around? Well, it is not so easy. One thing that you can do is to decide if you really need things that come in aerosol cans. Try to think of ways to make your life simpler by using less stuff. For example, you could open the windows when it gets stuffy inside.

Also, you can try to keep informed. Read the newspapers. There are plenty of publications put out by concerned people who will let you know if you are committing any crimes against nature when you shop at the supermarket.

There are many things you can do in your own house that have a positive impact on the world around you. For instance, you can save a whole tree by recycling 120 pounds of newspapers.

Everything you do has some impact, one way or the other.

144